MILITARY POSTS IN THE
POWDER RIVER COUNTRY OF WYOMING,
1865–1894

Military Posts in the Powder River Country of Wyoming, 1865–1894

ROBERT A. MURRAY

UNIVERSITY OF NEBRASKA PRESS·LINCOLN

Publishers on the Plains
UNP

MANUFACTURED IN THE UNITED STATES OF AMERICA

Dedicated to the seldom credited Sergeants and Corporals of the Regular Army, who trained the raw recruits of 1866, and thereby contributed to carrying the limited war in the Powder River country to its successful conclusion. In the words of Rudyard Kipling, a master observer of frontier armies: "... the backbone of the army is the non-commissioned man!"

Preface

The military posts in the Powder River country of Wyoming have long been left in the shadow of the dramatic conflicts which took place there. The Fetterman fight, the Wagon Box fight, Mackenzie's fight on the Red Fork, and the Johnson County Invasion have so attracted the attention of historians that they have obscured a good view of the military posts in most histories, and a good view of the background in which the conflicts themselves took place.

Part I of this book deals with the posts of the 1865–1868 period; sets forth the context in which they functioned, their structural history, and resources; and summarizes operations based upon them during this period of limited warfare.

Part II deals in like manner with the very different posts of the 1876–1894 period. In this era the Indian was driven from the region and the open-range cattle industry rose and fell. The era ends as the foundation was laid for today's land-use pattern in the region.

Supplementing both parts are appendices and notes giving data and sources of interest for the serious student, along with an extensive collection of maps, plans, drawings, and photos.

It is a great pleasure, at the end of this four-year project, to remember the many valuable professional contacts that grew out of it, and the great respect I gained for those who helped to enrich my knowledge. One of my greatest fears is that someone may be left out: I hope that there will not be many of them.

Special thanks are due to the Wyoming State Historical Society for the research grant that made this book possible; to the Wyoming State Parks Commission, which has jurisdiction over the Fort Reno site and parts of the Fort Philip Kearny and Wagon Box fight sites, who extended every possible assistance and courtesy; to the Bureau of Land Management, which controls the Cantonment Reno site; to the Western History Research Center of the University of Wyoming; and last, but far from least, to the Wyoming State Archives and Historical Department and its sister agency, the Wyoming State Library.

The National Archives and Records Service, prime source for the documentary materials used, was always prompt, courteous, and efficient in answering my many requests, with increasingly tighter deadlines to work under as the project moved along. Mr. Victor Gondos and his entire staff, who work with early army records, deserve special mention. Mr. Elmer O. Parker, Mr. Garry D. Ryan, and Mr. A. P. Muntz were helpful, patient, and encouraging beyond the requirements of good service.

Miss Lola M. Homsher and Mr. Neal E. Miller of the Wyoming State Archives and Historical Department were particularly encouraging and helpful, and Mrs. Katherine Halverson of the Department's Historical Division was always ready to make an efficient search for important fragments needed at inconvenient times.

Others deserving special mention are: Mr. Paul Henderson of Bridgeport, Nebraska; Mr. Burton S. Hill, Reverend Stuart Frazier, and Mrs. Thelma G. Condit of Buffalo, Wyoming; Mr. D. O. Geier of Banner, Wyoming; Mrs. Elsa Spear Byron, Mr. Glenn Sweem, Major Allen Bourne, and Mr. Charles Luxmoore of Sheridan; Mr. O. W. "Bill" Judge and Mr. Hans Larsen of Casper; Dr. T. A. Larson and Dr. Gene M. Gressley of the University of Wyoming at Laramie; Mr. John D. McDermott and Dr. Don Rickey, Jr., of Arlington, Virginia; and Mr. Tom Tisdale of Cheyenne.

My wife Marian served as Acting Commissary of Subsistence and Acting Quartermaster through the whole campaign, and endured both the field work and the waiting, much in the manner of the ladies of 1866. She also served as personnel data processor to keep the personalities in the book in their appropriate identity and relationship.

Mrs. Nancy Nash of Torrington, who typed the manuscript, was always alert for "typos and gremlins" in my own final draft.

ROBERT A. MURRAY

Contents

List of Figures

Part I
The Early Posts, 1865–1868

Chapter 1. The Stage for Limited Warfare, 1865–1868

The Civil War drew rapidly to a close in the early months of 1865, and the nation stirred in preparation for a vast quarter-century of westward movement. The West had not been neglected during the war years, but the government's attention was largely limited to ensuring the loyalty of the western states and territories and to maintaining essential lines of communication with them.

Conditions that had always facilitated westward movement were evident by early 1865. Within the population of the East were thousands, tired of war, but stirred by war-bred restlessness. Corporate and individual capital reserves to finance westward movement, and industrial and technological resources to open up and exploit the new land were both at an all-time high. An expanded urban-industrial segment of the economy required new raw materials and a larger food supply. Thus, both the motivating forces and the necessary resources existed for settlement of the frontier in this generation of "manifest destiny."

But westward expansion was hindered by the colorful and diverse Indian tribes of the Plains, who roamed and hunted over a broad belt of the new country. Themselves mostly newcomers to the Plains, the Indians were riding the crest of a dramatic two-hundred-year cultural change. Through trade, adoption, and innovation they were materially in a better position than ever to defend themselves and their interests. But technologically they were still a thousand years or more behind their white neighbors. In addition, they hardly possessed a functioning government, even at the hunting-band level, which was capable of dealing with their changing relationship with the white man. Tough, resourceful, individual fighters, these warriors of the Plains were hampered by their lack of organization and by their view of war itself. To the Indian, warfare was an essential and major factor in his way of life. Largely an individual road to social and economic success and spiritual merit, Plains tribal warfare possessed many of the surface aspects of the tribal raids of northern Europe in late Roman times, but in most circumstances lacked even that degree of organization. Even the Indians' largest forays were but collective vengeance raids, usually (but not always) seasonal, and frequently following the gathering of a number of hunting bands for religious purposes.[1]

By contrast, the Indians faced a white enemy to whom warfare was primarily a means of implementing group policy toward another group, to whom warfare was a fairly clear-cut alternative to a state of peace, and one in which group relations were conducted by a quite different set of rules. The Western European civilization, as extended to and adopted in North America, had long possessed a greater ability for formal organization than the Plains tribes. Even the small white frontier communities of the first quarter of the nineteenth century were better organized, more cooperative in peace, and better disciplined in war than the Plains Indian in his own kind of continuous warfare. Thus, the Plains Indian in 1865 faced a nation to whom warfare was no longer a game, but a highly organized and specialized industry, to be set in motion as the dictates of policy required.[2]

The tribes dominating the northern and central Plains and the eastern Rockies were caught between two frontiers of white settlement. That in the East, resembling earlier American frontiers, was a fairly continuous line of reasonably self-sufficient agricultural settlements, pressing steadily westward and moving slowly enough to maintain good internal lines of communication and transportation. This line in 1865 ran from central Minnesota down through southeastern Dakota Territory, then to the Platte, a hundred miles above its mouth, and continued through the Blue River country and across Kansas to the Indian Territory. The other frontier was eastward moving in general, and was based on settlements of the 1840's and 1850's in the Pacific Coast valleys and around Salt Lake. A complex and noncontinuous frontier, it advanced by thrusting off into attractive mining or farming and ranching country and establishing enclaves

[1] See especially Frank R. Secoy, *Changing Military Patterns on the Great Plains* (Locust Valley, N.Y.: American Ethnological Society, 1953); and Frank G. Roe, *The Indian and the Horse* (Norman: University of Oklahoma Press, 1955).

[2] Walter Millis, *Arms and Men* (New York: New American Library, 1958), pp. 64–116.

which sought to maintain communications, modernize their towns rapidly, and open up the commercial routes that would ensure economic survival and development. There were two such settlements on the fringe of Plains Indian territory in 1865: the mining region lying in a half-circle west of Denver, and the sprawling array of mining towns in the valleys of southwestern Montana.[3]

The westward-moving frontier on the Plains constantly displaced tribes of that region. Some of them were forced southward to Indian Territory. Others, such as the Sioux, were crowded westward to country already heavily hunted by relatives and old enemies alike.[4]

Between these two frontiers were strung lines of communication and transportation, important to the survival and economic growth of the western settlements. Commercial interests and government agencies of both frontier regions sought the protection and development of these routes, for it was primarily there that the Plains Indians and the white population of the two frontiers came into frequent conflict. Before 1865, the characteristic pattern of conflict with the Plains tribes was the incident-reprisal sequence. A classic case, the Grattan incident on August 19, 1854, stimulated a sizable punitive expedition under General William S. Harney, which culminated in the destruction of a Sioux camp on the Blue Water on September 3, 1855. Such also were the campaigns in western Kansas in the late fifties, and the Minnesota Sioux Uprising and its two punitive expeditions.[5]

By 1865, many observers perceived the fundamental inadequacies of this incident-reprisal sequence. Westerners hoped for a more decisive military settlement of the Indian question, a hope not to be realized for a dozen years. Those not so directly concerned sought a more humanitarian, peaceful solution in the often tried treatymaking process.

On the surface the potential for an effective military solution was high, with a massive army and a volume war production capability in

[3] Dale Van Every, *The Final Challenge* (New York: New American Library, 1964), pp. 335–359.

[4] See George Hyde, *Red Cloud's Folk* (Norman: University of Oklahoma Press, 1937); Hyde, *Spotted Tail's Folk* (Norman: University of Oklahoma Press, 1960); Hyde, *Pawnee Indians* (Denver: University of Denver Press, 1951). All discuss many of the phenomena of tribal displacement.

[5] C. M. Oehler, *The Great Sioux Uprising* (New York: Oxford University Press, 1959); LeRoy R. Hafen and Ann W. Hafen, editors, *Relations with the Indians of the Plains, 1857–1861* (Glendale, California: The Arthur H. Clark Co., 1959); Lloyd E. McCann, "The Grattan Massacre," *Nebraska History*, XXXVII, Number 1 (March 1956); Hyde, *Spotted Tail's Folk*.

existence. Actually, the nation, by the opening months of 1865, was tired of war, and the war machine was destined to disappear with astonishing rapidity. The occupation of the southern states and the manning of coastal defenses left only a part of the diminishing army available for frontier service. With only the experience of the early punitive expeditions to draw upon, there were few officers who understood Plains warfare. Logistic support for large-scale operations remained a formidable problem wherever wagon transport was involved.

Prospects for peace with the Plains tribes looked good to those who did not know the Indians, the country, or the complex interests of the westerners. The myth of the Great American Desert died hard: wishful thinkers felt it was an ideal abode for the Indian while his acculturation proceeded. The irrationality of negotiating, signing, and ratifying formal treaties with a people whose government was incapable of enforcing a treaty on its own members was not entirely unknown, but was generally unappreciated. Those far removed in distance or in time from the frontier experience could scarcely conceive that a government which had recently beaten many states into submission could not, politically or militarily, control its people's westward movement any more successfully than the British and colonial governments had after 1763.

Westerners had first chance in this game of "how best to deal with the Indians." The Sioux Uprising in Minnesota, along with other unrelated incidents along routes of travel, were interpreted far and wide as a general war on the Plains. The punitive expeditions of General Alfred Sully, Colonel John M. Chivington, and General Kit Carson accomplished little but to complicate and intensify the incident-reprisal sequence on the Plains and to increase danger to the very lines of communication and transportation whose safety were the main concern at this time.[6]

Several of these routes of travel and communication in 1865 are of prime concern in this book. The old Platte Valley, Sweetwater, and South Pass route of Oregon, California, and Mormon trail fame still served as a freight and immigrant road at the beginning of 1865. The alternate Overland route through southern Wyoming, shorter but more difficult, was the main mail, stage, and telegraph road, and also handled some wagon freight. Maintenance of these central, easy-gradient passes to the West was a clear-cut matter of national interest,

[6] *Ibid.*

upon which there was no disagreement. Secondary and more contro-
versial were the Bozeman Trail, which in 1863 was plotted to extend
from Bridger's Ferry on the North Platte River, along the east of and
around the north end of the Big Horn Mountains, and over one low
pass to Bozeman, the eastern gateway to the Montana mining districts; and the Bridger Trail, which left the North Platte at Platte
Bridge (Fort Caspar), ran northwest to the south end of the Big
Horns, over a moderate pass, and on through the dry Big Horn Basin,
joining the Bozeman Trail on the Yellowstone. Not yet much used,
but thought to have future importance, were trails up the Yellowstone
from its head of navigation, and overland from the mouth of the
Niobrara, joining the Bozeman Trail in the Powder River country.[7]

These secondary trails were useful mainly to the Montana mining
country at their western terminus, and to mercantile interests at and
around their eastern points of departure. Montana citizens and their
sympathizers throughout the West promoted all these routes vigorously as a matter of vital local interest, although none of them were
arteries upon which Montana depended for survival. Throughout the
sixties and seventies, Montana's heavy commercial traffic moved up
and down the Missouri River, to and from Fort Benton, which was
connected to the mining districts by relatively short trails. Multitudes
of persons used the same route for safety and convenience. The sole
disadvantage of the river route was its slowness. Light freight and
express traffic, along with stagecoach traffic, served the region by
branching off the old Overland route in Utah and heading north over
an easy pass to Montana.

The secondary roads were of value mainly to emigrants who sought
to reach Montana reasonably quickly with their stock and wagons at a
minimum cash outlay, and to those miners who wanted a speedy
shortcut out of Montana, and who could travel light at minimum cost
with their own outfits. The secondary trails were thus not of vital
national interest, though westerners talked as though they were. The
Bozeman and Bridger trails, although shorter than the Utah-Idaho
route, did not compete with steamboat traffic on the Missouri River
in terms of the cost-of-freight-shipment. Costs per pound over these
trails ran twice that of river freight plus the short wagon run from the

[7] See J. Cecil Alter, *James Bridger* (Columbus, Ohio: Longs, 1951); Grace
Raymond Hebard and E. A. Brininstool, *The Bozeman Trail* (Glendale, California:
The Arthur H. Clark Co., 1960); Burton S. Hill, "Bozeman and the Bozeman
Trail," *Annals of Wyoming*, XXXVI (October 1964), 204–233.

river ports. The presence of hostile Indians along the Bozeman Trail and the lack of forage and water on much of the Bridger Trail were secondary considerations that helped to eliminate them as light express and passenger routes in this period.[8]

*A real factor of national interest in early 1865 was the transcontinental railroad. Incidents along the main westward trails in 1863 and 1864 were cast as portents of trouble for surveyors and construction crews when the railroad line started west. The Secretary of the Interior, in January, 1865, called the attention of the Secretary of War to the importance of the railroad and endorsed the removal of Indians from the valleys of the Platte and Republican rivers. He went on to encourage the army to have General P. E. Connor extend his operations as far east as the Blue River country of Nebraska.[9]

Lieutenant Colonel William O. Collins, who was familiar with incidents along the Oregon and Overland trails outlined his views of the situation in a lengthy report on February 15, 1865:

> . . . the permanent cure for the hostilities of the Northern Indians is to go into the heart of their buffalo country and hold forts until the trouble is over. A hasty expedition, however successful, is only a temporary lesson, whereas the presence of troops in force in the country where the Indians are compelled to live and subsist would soon oblige them to sue for peace and accept such terms as the government may think proper to impose. . . . There are two points I would respectfully indicate as suitable locations for the posts spoken of, one about the head of the Little Missouri of the Mandans near the Three Buttes, and the other at some proper place on Powder River.[10]

Collins appears to be the first army advocate of abandoning the purely punitive policy toward the Indians in this region, and the first to suggest occupation as a means of minimizing depredations along the primary routes of travel.

Within a week after receiving Collins' report, General R. B. Mitchell proposed to strike at the Indians in the Powder River country, but it is not evident that he had more than a punitive expedition in mind.[11]

[8] The economics of transportation to Montana are thoroughly explored in William E. Lass, *Steamboating on the Upper Missouri* (Lincoln: University of Nebraska Press, 1962), pp. 39–51.

[9] J. P. Upsher, Secretary of the Interior to Edwin B. Stanton, Secretary of War, January 12, 1865, *War of the Rebellion*, Ser. I, XLVIII, Pt. 1, 498–499.

[10] Report of Lieutenant Colonel William O. Collins, 11th Ohio Volunteer Cavalry, February 15, 1865, 54th Cong., 1st Sess., H. Doc. 369, Pt. I, p. 98.

[11] Telegram, Brigadier General R. B. Mitchell to Major General Grenville M. Dodge, February 23, 1865, *War of the Rebellion*, Ser. I, XLVIII, Pt. 1, p. 961; telegram, Dodge to Mitchell, February 23, 1865, *ibid.*; telegram, Mitchell to Dodge, February 24, 1865, *ibid.*, p. 971.

Major General Grenville M. Dodge inquired, "Where is Powder River, and how far from Julesburg?"[12]—probably the last time anyone in authority in the West had to ask that question, as the year's activities spotlighted the Powder River region for the nation.

The army reorganized its western forces to bring the troubled area under one command on March 28, 1865, when the former Districts of Nebraska, Utah, and Colorado were merged into the single District of the Plains, under Brigadier General P. E. Connor, with head-quarters at Denver.[13] Connor assumed command on March 30, 1865,[14] and from then until late September he directed most operations in the District. Connor's main effort was the Powder River Expedition, basically an outgrowth of the plan suggested by Lieutenant Colonel Collins in February. The Hafens have ably presented most of the data on this expedition, and it need be presented here only in outline.[15]

Connor's expedition was in the planning stage when Colonel Thomas Moonlight of the Kansas Volunteers led the last conventional punitive strike, which spent itself in a fruitless march from Fort Laramie to the Wind River country. Moonlight's forces did little but expend manpower, transport, and matériel that might better have been conserved at this time.

Detailed plans for the Powder River Expedition changed frequently through the spring of 1865. All, however, envisioned a multipronged drive into the Indian country from various points in an effort to seek out and destroy hostile bands, to overawe those Indians who would not fight, and to build at least two permanent posts for occupation of the region. Truly, on paper, this was a real test of the western thesis on pacifying the northern Plains tribes.

Problems arose continuously as the expedition assembled. Rapid demobilization of the volunteer units, along with federal economy moves, cut the proposed manpower drastically. The four columns of the expedition, assembled at their points of departure, totaled only 2,072 men. The troops were well armed and well supplied with ammunition, but the quality and quantity of food, forage, and transport were poor from the start. Considering the population of the region, none of the columns captured significant numbers of Indians,

[12] Telegram, Dodge to Mitchell, February 23, 1865, *War of the Rebellion*, Ser. I, XLVIII, Pt. 1, 961.

[13] General Order Number 80, Headquarters, Department of the Missouri, St. Louis, Missouri, March 28, 1865, NARS, RG98, Department of the Missouri.

[14] General Order Number 1, Headquarters, District of the Plains, issued at Fort Kearny, Nebraska Territory, March 30, 1865, NARS, RG98, District of the Plains.

[15] LeRoy R. Hafen and Ann W. Hafen, *The Powder River Campaigns and Sawyer's Expedition, 1865* (Glendale, California: The Arthur H. Clark Co., 1961).

although the columns themselves were frequently harassed by Sioux and Cheyenne war parties. Only one engagement of consequence took place—the destruction of an Arapaho village near present-day Ranchester, Wyoming, on August 29, 1865.

The expedition broke up in September, 1865, having two lasting effects: first, the animosity of the Sioux and Cheyennes, and their contempt for the white soldier; and second, the establishment in August, 1865, of Fort Connor (soon to be renamed Fort Reno) on the Powder River.[16] Thus, except for the establishment of this post, the expedition amounted merely to a sizable and largely unsuccessful punitive expedition of the old pattern.

The military effort to pacify the northern Plains tribes having proved largely ineffective, the Peace party came forward with its own ideas for dealing with the tribes. This faction found new support and new energy in late 1865. The Civil War was over; the lunatic fringe, which had thrived on the antislavery crusade and had attempted to dominate the war to save the Union, found itself morally unemployed. They had little interest in the tough and worldly problems of peace and reconstruction, and were casting about for new crusades. Some chose woman suffrage, others temperance, but many joined the various groups that the westerners unkindly lumped together as "Indian lovers."[17]

Other important forces at work in the 1866 negotiations with the Plains tribes were westerners who wished to develop all possible routes of communication and transportation in order to improve their economic position, along with promoters at the eastern terminii of these routes. There were those who wanted to finish the Indian question as a military problem as quickly as possible, in order to facilitate the opening up and development of the region. There were those who advocated forced Indian removal to distant reservations, either to open up the land or to force Indian acculturation. Some wanted to guarantee the Indians their present territory indefinitely, to provide time for them to adjust to acculturation; while others wanted to restrict progressively their territory in order to force their acculturation; and still others who wished to preserve the *status quo*

[16] *Ibid.*

[17] For a good discussion of the alignment of forces in the peace movement of this period, see Henry E. Fritz, *The Movement for Indian Assimilation, 1860–1890* (Philadelphia: University of Pennsylvania Press, 1963); and Robert G. Athearn, *William Tecumseh Sherman and the Settlement of the West* (Norman: University of Oklahoma Press, 1956).

simply to exploit the Indian trade. Some people wished to avoid the high cost of an Indian war; others regarded an Indian war as unfeasible in view of other army commitments. Last were those who wished to promote railroad construction as the immediate economic answer and the ultimate strategic answer to the Indian question. All of these factors were at work in the evolution of a scheme for some kind of treaty with the hostile northern Plains tribes in 1865–1866. The course of action resulting from such complex interests could only be an uncomfortable compromise, satisfactory only to small portions of the Indian or the white population.

Commissioners drew up a set of treaties to limit the Indians to a definite territory away from the critical east-west routes of travel, and to provide for travel along supplemental routes through the Indian country. In return the Indians were to receive substantial presents and various inducements to acculturation. Only a few Indians signed the agreements, and these were of varying importance. A large body of Indian spokesmen walked out of the negotiations. A sizable number of presents were distributed to secure signatures, with little result. Finally, Congress refused to ratify the treaties and they did not take effect.[18]

To pacify western interests, the army prepared to bolster the vociferously supported Bozeman Trail with several more army posts. Their garrisons were ordered to protect travel, but not to provoke a general Indian war. In this difficult situation, the army held the upper hand throughout, and grew tactically stronger day by day. Logistic support remained the army's most important problem in executing its assigned duties throughout this period, but daily the final answer—the Union Pacific Railroad—crept westward, slashing transportation costs and speeding the movement of men and matériel to the end of the track. General William T. Sherman looked forward eagerly to its completion, which would render obsolete the old posts scattered along the secondary trails.

The regular regiments, thrust into the Powder River country in the wake of the Connor campaign, had few officers experienced in Indian warfare. Their enlisted strength consisted largely of new recruits and

[18] For discussions of the unsuccessful negotiations of 1866, see the *Montana Post* (Virginia City, Montana), July 7, 1866; letters from James Brennan in *The Daily Union Vedette* (Salt Lake City, Utah Territory), June 8, 1866, June 24, 1866, June 29, 1866, and editorial comment on same, August 17, 1866; James C. Olson, *Red Cloud and the Sioux Problem* (Lincoln: University of Nebraska Press, 1965), pp. 27–40; and Athearn, *William Tecumseh Sherman and the Settlement of the West*, pp. 65–71.

their best officers and men had had Civil War experience, which was of limited value on the Plains. Training was poor and the equipment was often left over from the Civil War. In spite of this, the army still possessed a coherent purpose and a degree of organization and discipline that exceeded that of the Indian, and gave the troops a constant tactical advantage, thrown away only once—in the Fetterman Fight of December 21, 1866.

The Plains Indians, on the other hand, possessed no strategic concept. They were so disunited that they could seldom cooperate for tactical purposes. Those whose long contact with the white man gave them a glimpse of their position vis-à-vis the United States government kept the peace and maneuvered with their agents and with the army for such advantages as they could gain.

During the early period of the Powder River posts the regular army could not muster political support for the major campaign that some westerners wanted. The Indians, on the other hand, could not seriously menace the posts and their lines of supply. Under these conditions, only a state of what we today would call "limited warfare" could prevail.

The Bozeman Trail was an emigrant route, and so it remained, unable to compete economically with the river traffic, and clearly made obsolete when the railroads in 1868 reached the heads of competitive trails farther west. Since no practical political or economic advantage remained, the trail could thus be abandoned to the eager Indian and his eastern champions, while the army withdrew to its new and more efficient posts on the railroad line and bolstered its advanced bases, Fort Fetterman and Fort Laramie, outside the Indian reservation created in 1868. (This reservation included that portion of Dakota Territory between the Missouri River and the 104th meridian. The lands west of the reservation and east of the Big Horns were left unceded, as a hunting area for the tribes of the region.)

Fort Reno (Fort Connor) and Fort Philip Kearny lived out their existence, then, in this context. The story of these two posts forms the body of Part I of this book.

Chapter 2. Structural History of Fort Reno (Fort Connor)

Lieutenant Colonel William O. Collins, 11th Ohio Volunteer Cavalry, in a report of February 15, 1865, suggested construction of a post "at some proper place on Powder River."[1] Major General Grenville M. Dodge envisioned such a post in his first instructions to General Connor.[2] Major General John Pope, commanding the Military Division of the Missouri, made it clear that he considered it Dodge's responsibility, and hence Connor's direct task, to "establish the post at Powder River."[3] Dodge suggested that "sufficient infantry to hold most of the posts will be sent you from the regiments raised from Confederate prisoners in our hands enlisted for service on the Plains."[4]

Dodge set forth criteria for location of the post on the Powder River on June 10, 1865:

> . . . In the location of a post on Powder River have in view the holding in check of the Indians, the possibility of obtaining forage, hay, wood, etc., and its position with reference to a route of travel to Montana, either from Fort Laramie or from some point east, as well as the roads coming west from the Missouri River.[5]

The Connor expedition leaving Fort Laramie on July 30, 1865, included six companies of the Sixth Michigan Volunteer Cavalry,

[1] Report of Lieutenant Colonel William O. Collins, February 15, 1866, *War of the Rebellion*, Ser. I, XLVIII, Pt. 1, p. 98.

[2] Telegram, Major General Grenville M. Dodge to General P. E. Connor, March 29, 1865, *War of the Rebellion*, Ser. I, XLVIII, Pt. 1, pp. 1295–1296.

[3] Major General John Pope to Dodge, June 3, 1865, *War of the Rebellion*, Ser. I, XLVIII, Pt. 1, 347.

[4] Dodge to Connor, March 29, 1865, *War of the Rebellion*, Ser. I, XLVIII, Pt. 1, pp. 1295–1296.

[5] Dodge to Connor, June 10, 1865, *War of the Rebellion*, Ser. I, XLVIII, Pt. 1, pp. 348–349.

Figure 1. Fort Reno, late 1866, from a sketch by M. D. Houghton. (*From A. B. Ostrander, The Bozeman Trail Forts Under General Philip St. George Cooke.*)

under Colonel James H. Kidd, intended as the troops who would build and garrison the post on the Powder.[6] The column struck out from the North Platte, following the general line of the Bozeman Trail, up and over the low rolling divides between a series of stream courses, and down to the Powder River. Connor had 745 officers, men, and civilian employees; 185 wagons, and over 1,600 horses and mules.[7] In order to secure adequate forage, sufficient water, and enough space, the command had to spread its camps for several miles along the bottom lands of the Powder. This dispersal of the camp— "Camp Connor"—has confused some students as to the exact location of Fort Connor. However, contemporary evidence,[8] especially the inspection report of Brevet Major General William B. Hazen (colonel of the yet-to-be-activated 38th Infantry), who visited the post on assignment as a special inspector in August, 1866, before the regulars started major new construction, leaves no doubt whatever on the matter of location. The site selected was near the center of Section 33, Township 45 North, Range 78 West.[9]

This site lies on a high bench, north (left bank) of the Powder. At this point the river flows due east for about one and a quarter miles. The edge of the bench with the fort site runs generally parallel to the course of the stream. Topographic maps show the location to be precisely fifty-six feet above the river level.[10]

Connor's men, beginning August 14, 1865, first built a small stockade, roughly 120 feet square. Cottonwood logs eight to ten inches thick were cut from standing timber across the Powder. These posts were set about four feet deep in a trench, leaving a wall about eight feet high.

They put up two buildings. One of these, soon filled with quartermaster's stores, was of cottonwood logs, thirty by ninety-six feet, with

[6] Captain H. E. Palmer, "Account of the Connor Expedition," in LeRoy R. Hafen and Ann W. Hafen, *The Powder River Campaigns and Sawyer's Expedition, 1865* (Glendale, California: The Arthur H. Clark Co., 1961), p. 109.

[7] *Ibid.*

[8] *Ibid.,* p. 117.

[9] Report of William B. Hazen to Adjutant General, Department of the Platte, sent from Fort Reno, August 22, 1866, NARS, RG98, LR, Department of the Platte; Henry B. Carrington, testimony in "Proceedings of a Court of Inquiry re: the Fetterman Massacre," special file GCMO–002236, Judge Advocate General's Records, NARS, RG153; Margaret I. Carrington, *Absaraka, Home of the Crows* (Chicago: Lakeside Press, 1950), pp. 106–107; William Murphy, "The Forgotten Battalion," *Annals of Wyoming,* VII, Number 2 (October 1930), 384; Van Voast (post commander at Fort Reno) in General Order Number 28, Headquarters, Fort Reno, September 1, 1867, NARS, RG98.

[10] United States Geological Survey Topographic Map, Fort Reno, Wyoming, 7.5 minute quadrangle, N4345–W10607.5/7.5, 1953.

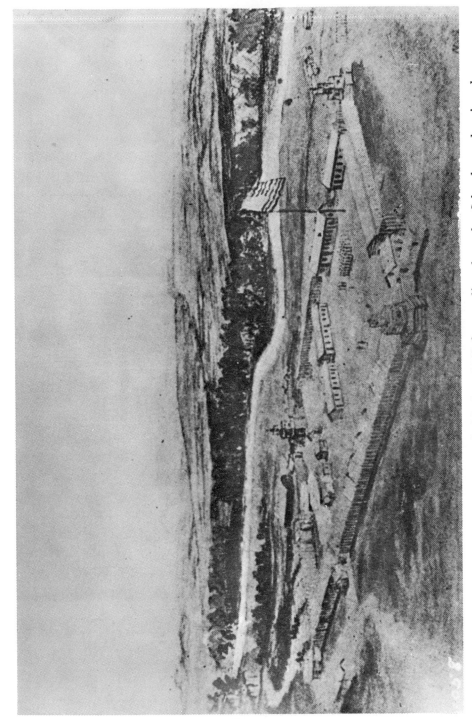

Figure 2. Sketch of Fort Reno, probably late 1867 but earlier than the Schonborn drawing, by Captain Proctor. (*Wyoming State Archives and Historical Department.*)

the front left open, and the roof and front covered with canvas. The other building, of the same dimensions, was a complete structure, with a pole and dirt roof.[11] The storehouses had not been finished on September 9 [12] but were probably completed by September 24, 1865, when one building outside the stockade was up, and more were under construction.[13]

The Sawyer Wagon Road outfit arrived at Fort Connor just after construction started, and their escort, Companies C and D, 5th U.S. Volunteers, replaced the Michigan Cavalry as garrison of the post.[14] About September 23, Company A, Omaha scouts (actually Winnebagos),[15] joined the garrison. This, then, was the force that completed the construction of Fort Connor.

The men built two barracks of unhewn cottonwood logs, chinked and mud-plastered. The buildings measured twenty-five by ninety feet each, and a space was partitioned off at one end of each barracks as a mess room. In common with most other buildings at Fort Connor, the roofs were made of cottonwood poles, supporting a covering of earth. They had rough floors, possibly puncheons, according to Hazen's description.

The post's two officers' quarters were of hewn cottonwood logs, twenty by thirty feet, and nine feet high. These structures had the same earth-covered roofs, but were dirt floored. Each of these two buildings was divided into three rooms.

Another hewn-log building housed the post hospital. This was twenty-five by thirty-three feet, and eight feet high. It also had a dirt roof, but Hazen does not mention a floor. He said:

> It has a single ward with about ten feet partitioned off at one end, in which is quartered the Surgeon, which is his dispensary, and in which he keeps all his stores and supplies. . . . Cooking is done in the ward, and although the hospital has a general cleanly appearance, I can conceive of but little additional comfort to anyone placed there.[16]

Hazen mentions structures used in 1866 as shops and as teamsters' quarters. These are probably buildings No. 8 and No. 9 on the plan

[11] Hazen, Report on Fort Reno, August 22, 1866.

[12] Captain B. F. Rockafellow, 6th Michigan Volunteer Cavalry, "Diary," in Hafen and Hafen, *Powder River Campaigns and Sawyer's Expedition*, p. 190.

[13] Lewis B. Hull, "Soldiering on the Plains," *Kansas Historical Quarterly*, VII, Number 1 (February 1938), 51.

[14] Rockafellow, "Diary," p. 186.

[15] Colonel Nelson Cole, Second Missouri Artillery, "Report," in Hafen and Hafen, *Powder River Campaigns and Sawyer's Expedition*, p. 88.

[16] This and most other precise descriptive material on early Fort Reno are from Hazen, Report on Fort Reno.

Figure 3. Drawing of Fort Reno, late 1867, from the southwest, by Anton Schonborn. (*National Archives and Records Service.*)

18

(Figure 5). During the volunteer period one of these may have served as quarters for the Winnebagos, but this is purely conjectural.

The name of the post was officially changed from Fort Connor to Fort Reno on November 11, 1865, but notice of the change did not reach the post for over a month.[17] There are no indications of additional work on the buildings during the volunteer occupancy: the men simply settled down and awaited mustering out.

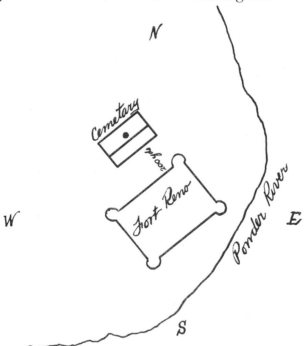

Figure 4. Sketch, done from memory by Lieutenant James McBride Stembel in 1878, showing the relative positions of Fort Reno and its cemetery. (*National Archives and Records Service.*)

Arrival of the Carrington column on June 28, 1866, relieved the volunteers, but left the fate of the post in doubt for some time. Carrington's original orders envisioned abandoning Fort Reno and establishing a new post of that name about forty miles up the road.[18] He organized his command with this in mind, but finding larger quantities of supplies at Fort Reno than he could transport, he left Company B, 2nd Battalion, 18th Infantry, under Captain Proctor

[17] General Order Number 46, Headquarters, Department of the Missouri, November 11, 1865, NARS, RG98. Post orders and correspondence were still headed "Fort Connor," well into December 1865.

[18] General Order Number 33, Headquarters, Department of the Missouri, March 10, 1866, NARS, RG98; Special Order Number 40, Headquarters, United States Forces, Kansas and the Territories, March 28, 1866, NARS, RG98.

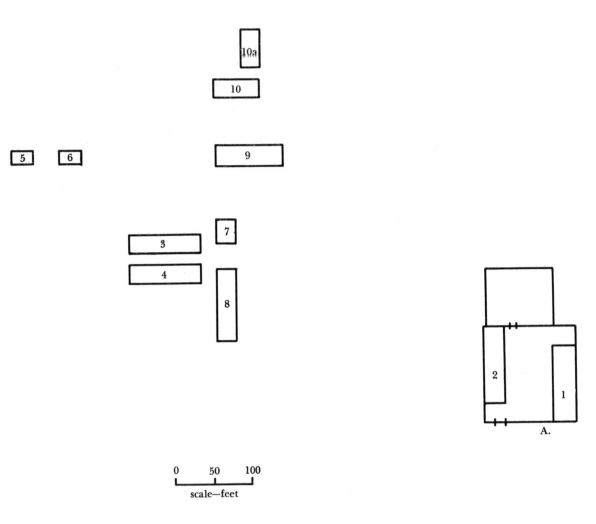

0   50   100

scale—feet

A. Log stockade around warehouses
1. Quartermaster's storehouse
2. Commissary storehouse
3. Barracks
4. Barracks
5. Officers' quarters
6. Officers' quarters
7. Post hospital
8. Shops
9. Teamsters' quarters (possibly used as a barracks for the Omaha Scouts)
10. Sutler's store, built by the A. C. Leighton firm, autumn, 1865
10a. A second sutler's building

Figure 5. Fort Reno, from its completion, in late 1865, until July, 1866.

there, and designated the post "Reno Station." [19] Unknown at this moment to Carrington, Headquarters, Department of the Platte, on June 28, 1866, issued new orders on the distribution of troops in the Mountain District. These orders specified that two companies were to garrison Fort Reno, which was to remain active.[20] Company G, 2nd Battalion, 18th Infantry, first re-enforced the Fort Reno garrison, but was soon replaced by Company F, 2nd Battalion, 18th Infantry.[21]

Those familiar with the almost frantic air of activity at Fort Philip Kearny in this period might expect a similar activity at Fort Reno, once the order not to move the post was received. But such was not the case. When Hazen arrived at Fort Reno in August, 1866, on his assignment as Acting Inspector General, he found Carrington's two companies under Proctor occupying the old buildings of the post. They had done little work of any kind. A carelessly constructed cottonwood stockade had been thrown up around the old garrison buildings, and another, immediately adjacent, had been put up around a space for stock (Figure 6). The men still used open pits for sinks, as had the volunteers before them, and sometimes "the men go over the banks quite near the post, and against the stockades at the calls of nature." [22] Hazen noted that the newer portion of the stockades built by Proctor's men was inferior to that around the quartermaster and commissary storehouses put up by the volunteers. He recommended that the stockade be taken up, cut to even lengths, re-aligned and reset, and that the two barracks be moved to a new location. He made lengthy recommendations for correcting many other deficiencies in the administration of the post, and probably made many more orally to Carrington on his arrival at Fort Philip Kearny.[23]

Proctor and his men must have set to work vigorously in response to Hazen's comments, for the post changed considerably in the next

[19] General Order Number 4, Headquarters, Mountain District, June 30, 1866, NARS, RG98; Muster Roll, 18th Infantry, for July 1866, NARS, RG94; General Order Number 2, Headquarters, Mountain District, June 28, 1866, NARS, RG98.
[20] General Order Number 7, Headquarters, Department of the Platte, June 28, 1866, NARS, RG98.
[21] Hazen, Report on Fort Reno, August 22, 1866.
[22] *Ibid.*
[23] *Ibid.*, plus accompanying notes and correspondence; also, surveyor's field book, Ambrose G. Bierce, "Route Maps of a Journey from Fort Laramie-Dakota Territory to Fort Benton-Montana Territory, 1886" (MS in the Bienecke Library, William Robertson Coe collection, Yale University).

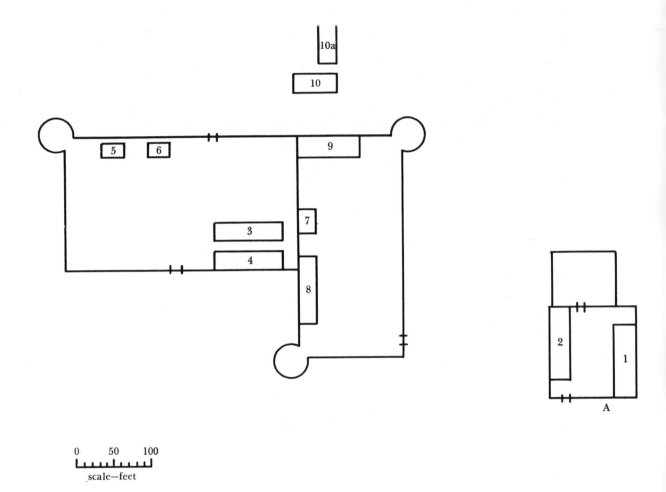

Figure 6. Fort Reno at the time of Hazen's inspection, August 21–22, 1866. Buildings are the same as in Figure 5. The new stockade had been erected by the men of the 18th Infantry between about August 5 and August 20, 1866. Hazen recommended that it be changed in outline and reset.

few months. In the repair of the stockade, they apparently left out the partition separating it into two units. They began other changes outlined on Figure 7.

Only one ground plan of the Fort Connor-Fort Reno continuum survives, so it is difficult to give precise stockade dimensions or exact building spacing. Hazen's civilian topographer, Ambrose G. Bierce, made a rough ground plan, and fortunately Hazen left good measurements and descriptions for the buildings he inspected. Major E. B. Grimes, Acting Quartermaster, who inspected the post late in 1867 left similar data on the new buildings of that period. In addition, there exist three good sketches of the post (Figures 1–3). From these sources, the author has compiled the sequence of ground plans shown on Figures 5, 6, 7, and 8. More accurate drawings must await a comprehensive archeological investigation, but these plans should be considered a fairly exact reference.

The early sketch (Figure 1) probably shows the Proctor-period work near completion. It agrees essentially with the descriptions of A. B. Ostrander, who arrived at Fort Reno on November 30, 1866.[24]

To complete the stockade, Proctor's men had added log bastions at its "northwest" and "southeast" corners (more nearly west and east, but in common with other frontier posts not precisely oriented, the army consistently used assumed directions in all descriptive material, orders, and correspondence). They built a sturdy adobe post commander's quarters, which lasted the lifetime of the post and serves to relate structural alignments to the later structures of the Van Voast period. Other buildings, all of cottonwood logs with dirt and pole roofs, are identified in the ground plans.

The long low building which Ostrander used as a combination living quarters and office may have been made simply by connecting building No. 5 and No. 6 to form building No. 13 (Figures 5, 6, and 7). Ostrander described the Adjutant's office as follows:

> It was a room about twelve by sixteen, with one door and one window, facing south. Army blankets had been spread on the dirt floor for a carpet. One long table on the west side of the room and a small desk near it, two chairs, and three or four camp stools completed the furniture. Nails were driven into the logs to hang coats and hats on.[25]

[24] A. B. Ostrander, *An Army Boy of the Sixties* (Chicago: World Book Company, 1926), pp. 137–142, 144.
[25] *Ibid.*, p. 145.

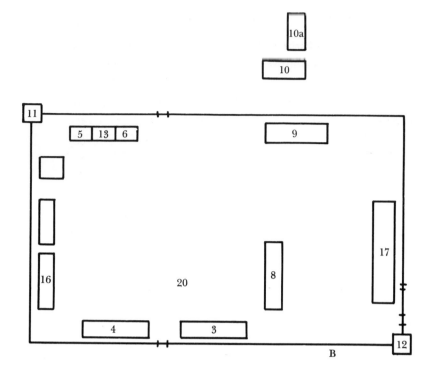

0   50   100
scale—feet

A. Stockade around warehouses, constructed in 1865 by Companies C and D, 5th U.S. Volunteers
B. Stockade around other buildings, as realigned and reset by Companies B and F, 18th Infantry, in accordance with Hazen's recommendations
1. Quartermaster's storehouse
2. Commissary storehouse
3. Barracks
4. Barracks
8. Possibly the same structure as building No. 8 in Figure 6. It may have been converted to laundresses' quarters by this time.
9. Possibly teamsters' quarters
10. Sutler's building
10a. Sutler's building
11. Blockhouse
12. Blockhouse
13. Officers' quarters and office building, possibly made by connecting buildings No. 5 and 6 of Figure 6
14. Post commander's quarters
15. Possibly civilian employees' quarters
16. Possibly a storehouse
17. Storehouse, shops, or stables
18. Quartermaster's office
19. Possibly teamsters' quarters
20. Flagstaff

Figure 7. Fort Reno, late 1866 and early 1867.

Ostrander's own quarters were in an adjacent room, which he describes as

> ... a room even a little larger than the office. The floor there also was of dirt, packed down hard. At the left, close to the doorway, was a small stand with a tin washbasin and a tin pan of soap on it. A towel hung on a nail above, and underneath was a bucket of water with a tin dipper handy. Just beyond and tight up in the corner was a bunk built up about two feet high.
>
> ... I went over and found a blanket had been doubled over, stuffed with hay, and the two ends and side roughly fastened with cord; and indeed it was a dandy mattress. Just below the foot of my bunk, and beginning about five feet from the floor, was a square window, which was curtained by a blanket at night.
>
> ... But the east side of the room was its most interesting part. It was mainly a great open fireplace, occupying a space of nearly six feet across and at least four feet deep, and rounded up to a height of about five feet. I looked up the chimney and saw a flue about two feet square almost to the top. I found afterward that more than half of the chimney was built up outside the line of the building.[26]

Mrs. Margaret Carrington, Colonel Carrington's wife, mentions a magazine built by Proctor,[27] however this does not conclusively appear on any of the views of the post, and is not mentioned by Grimes in his inspection report.

Early orders to Carrington indicate that there was a water-powered sawmill, possibly out of order, at Fort Reno.[28] We have no evidence that this was put to use, but by Ostrander's time a steam sawmill was in operation (Figure 1). It was situated on the river bottom at the foot of the bluff, along with several other structures. The strip of low ground on which these buildings stood has long since been eroded by the overactive Powder.

The energetic and resourceful Major James Van Voast assumed command of Fort Reno on June 30, 1867,[29] and soon after he began a series of major changes and improvements. By July 18, 1867, details were at work cutting timber "for the log quarters now being erected."[30]

[26] *Ibid.*

[27] Margaret Carrington, *Absaraka*, p. 107.

[28] Special Order Number 40, Headquarters, United States Forces, Kansas and the Territories, March 28, 1866, NARS, RG 98.

[29] General Order Number 18, Headquarters, Fort Reno, June 30, 1867, NARS, RG 98.

[30] Special Order Number 51, Headquarters, Fort Reno, July 18, 1867, NARS, RG 98.

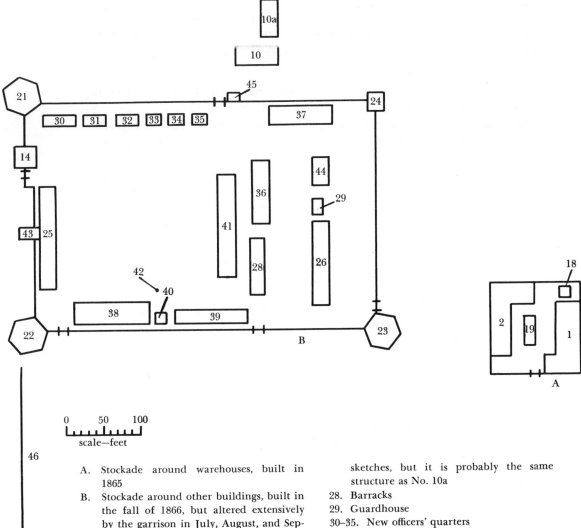

Figure 8. Fort Reno, November, 1867.

26

A. Stockade around warehouses, built in 1865

B. Stockade around other buildings, built in the fall of 1866, but altered extensively by the garrison in July, August, and September, 1867

1. Quartermaster's storehouse
2. Commissary storehouse
10. Sutler's store; building No. 10a may be the same building shown by Schonborn (see No. 27, below)
14. Commanding officer's quarters
18. Quartermaster's office
19. Possibly teamsters' quarters
21–23. New hexagonal blockhouses
24. New square blockhouse
25. Barracks
26. Corn storehouse
27. Cabin behind sutler's store as shown by
• Schonborn. This does not appear on all

sketches, but it is probably the same structure as No. 10a

28. Barracks
29. Guardhouse
30–35. New officers' quarters
36. Hospital
37. Quartermaster's storehouse
38. Barracks
39. Barracks
40. Cellar (magazine?) (Schonborn)
41. Possible location of last barracks (post-Schonborn)
42. New flagstaff, September, 1867
43. Cellar
44. Shop or office
45. Building outside gate, its use not known, possibly a sentry box (Schonborn)
46. Stockade-fence, about six feet high, extending toward the bluff, possibly used to help corral beef herds and wagon stock

Van Voast's first change seems to have been to tear down the long, partitioned combination office and quarters of Ostrander's time, and replace it with the six new log quarters shown (Figure 8). The old log barracks were torn down and replaced with larger structures, and three additional barracks were built by early November.

Van Voast relocated the entire west stockade line, tore down the old bastions, and built three new hexagonal blockhouses and a new square bastion, and relocated several of the gates. A guardhouse, additional warehouses, and new sinks substantially completed the work. The Anton Schonborn drawing of Fort Reno (Figure 3) is effectively dated in late 1867 by the fact that there are some buildings pictured which had not been completed before September 1, 1867, and there are several major buildings *not* pictured that were standing and completed, and were measured by Major Grimes on November 11 and 12, 1867.[31] Through all these changes, the old Connor quartermaster stockade stood undisturbed, with only improvements and additions to its warehouses, and the addition of two small structures (Figures 1–8). Grimes suggested that if the post was to be retained, all the cottonwood log structures should be replaced with adobe buildings.[32]

There is no evidence of additional building before the post was abandoned in 1868. Fire, whether started by Indians, lightning, or the ever dangerous prairie fire, appears to have destroyed much of the post after its abandonment. The writer has examined considerable amounts of charred wood and well-preserved pieces of chinking that appear to have been burned, both from the area of the officers' quarters. The site was marked for years by chimneys, bits of adobe wall, and heaps of iron from abandoned equipment. The larger pieces of evidence have gradually disappeared, but the area is still covered with many small bits of debris, much of it found on examination to be from the army post of the 1860's.

[31] Major E. B. Grimes to Chief Quartermaster, Department of the Platte, "Inspection Report of Fort Reno," November 11 and 12, 1867 (sent from Fort Laramie, December 2, 1867), NARS, RG 98, LR, Department of the Platte; General Order Number 28, Headquarters, Fort Reno, September 1, 1867, NARS, RG 98.

[32] Grimes, "Inspection Report of Fort Reno."

Chapter 3. Structural History of Fort Philip Kearny

Structurally, Fort Philip Kearny is distinctive in several respects. It was one of the largest truly fortified posts of the post-Civil War Indian country. It did not grow haphazardly in the manner of many other forts, but was designed, engineered, and carried to basic completion under the supervision of one man—Colonel Henry B. Carrington, 18th U.S. Infantry.

When Carrington received orders to construct new posts along the Bozeman Trail, he was still in winter quarters at Fort Kearny, Nebraska. He immediately requisitioned the necessary tools, equipment, and construction materials, and by April 26, 1866, he stated he had "proper tools for the erection of quarters and defenses," and "good instruments, transit and level." [1] Margaret Carrington makes note of "shingle and brick machines, doors, sash, glass, nails, locks, and every conceivable article that can enter into housebuilding." [2]

Most of the supplies and equipment arrived at Fort Philip Kearny without incident either with the column or on following trains, but the first of the steam sawmills was wrecked in the downslope runaway of its bull team, probably at Ash Hollow, Nebraska. [3] There is no indication that the equipment to make shingles for the steam sawmills arrived during Carrington's time, since numerous references show that Carrington's men made shingles with froes.

[1] Henry B. Carrington, statement in Senate Executive Document 33, 50th Congress, 1st Session, p. 2; Carrington to Adjutant General, Department of the Platte, April 26, 1866, NARS, RG 98, LR, Department of the Platte.

[2] Margaret I. Carrington, *Absaraka, Home of the Crows* (Chicago: Lakeside Press, 1950), p. 37.

[3] William Murphy, "The Forgotten Battalion," *Annals of Wyoming*, VII, Number 2 (October 1930), 383.

The Carrington column arrived on the Piney at eleven o'clock on the morning of July 13, 1866.[4] Carrington spent the next day, July 14, in the field with three officers, Guide Jim Bridger, and twenty mounted men. They examined a number of possible sites, some as far away as Goose Creek and the Tongue River. Returning to the expedition camp that night, Carrington concluded that the best spot available for construction of the post was at the forks of the Piney.[5] The area selected lies on a sloping bench, low in relation to the surrounding hills, but sharply elevated above the flood plains of the forks of the Piney on each side. Its exact location is the Southwest Quarter, Section 26, Township 53 North, Range 83 West of the 6th Principal Meridian, with some of the outlying buildings on adjacent quarter-sections.

Early on the morning of Sunday, July 15, Carrington, Captain Tenodor Ten Eyck, and the pioneer party set to work surveying and staking out the general lines of the post.[6] Following the survey, Carrington had loaded wagons drive around the street laid out surrounding the parade ground to pack it firmly.[7] The command then moved its tent camp to the site in careful order.[8] A horse-powered sawmill brought with the group was set up on the same day, and Carrington had work details organized to begin construction.[9]

It was probably at this time that Carrington finished and labeled his last preconstruction plan (Figure 9), based on drawings done while he was still at Fort Kearny, Nebraska. But Carrington soon became convinced that the post would have to be larger than he had envisioned. He accordingly modified the plan referred to above (Figure 9), and in general followed one with precise drawings made at the site (Figure 11). Before leaving Fort Philip Kearny, Carrington indicated on this plan work not completed and work not yet begun (see notes on plan, Figure 11).

During construction, all units, offices, officers and their families camped in tents until their respective buildings were completed, thus there was a gradual transition from tent camp to completed post (see

[4] Record of Events, Post Return for July, 1866, Fort Philip Kearny, NARS, RG 98.

[5] Henry B. Carrington, statement in Senate Executive Document 33, 50th Cong., 1st Sess., p. 9.

[6] *Ibid.*; Margaret Carrington, *Absaraka*, p. 121.

[7] Carrington, *Absaraka*, p. 121.

[8] *Ibid.*, pp. 121–122.

[9] *Ibid.*, pp. 122–123.

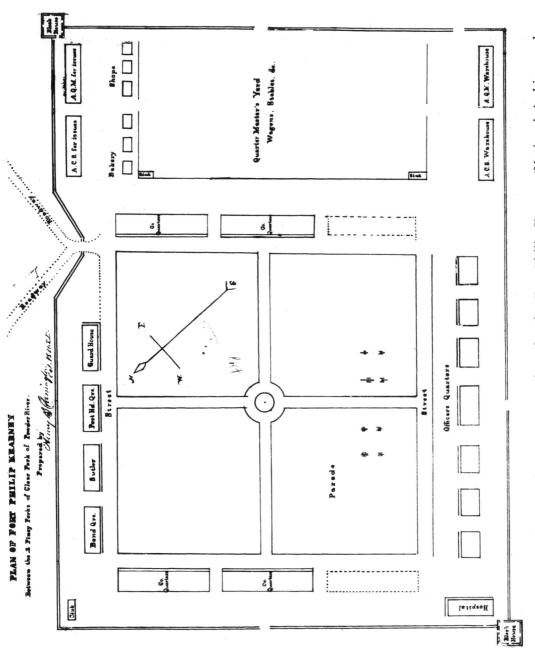

Figure 9. Garrington's last preconstruction plan for Fort Philip Kearny. (*National Archives and Records Service.*)

Figure 10). This sketch, submitted with Hazen's report, shows the post during the transitional stage, on August 28 or 29, 1866.

Working from Carrington's final plan (Figure 11), and all available construction data, the author has prepared a supplemental "as-built" ground plan of the post as of late December, 1866 (Figure 12). (Building numbers have been arbitrarily assigned as in the case of Fort Reno, to facilitate references and discussion.)

As mentioned before, Carrington acted as his own engineer, draftsman, and construction superintendent, although he did delegate the organization of some construction activities to the post commander, Captain Ten Eyck. Carrington was not well supplied with versatile and energetic officers, and it was perhaps in part because of this that he became overly preoccupied with building the fort and neglected many problems in his command. Later, he was much criticized for this.[10] However, his preoccupation did assure completion of the work with greater care than at some of the other western posts, and unquestionably made the fort as it stood in December, 1866—when he stopped construction—"Carrington's Fort" in concept, design, and detail.

In contrast to Fort Reno, Fort Philip Kearny had within a moderate radius large supplies of good building materials, as the following accounts describe:

> Limestone is attainable from the mountains, although somewhat difficult of transportation at present. Clay is abundant, and of such quality as to make a firm plaster coating upon simple exposure to the sun.
> . . . All other building materials are plentiful, and the tall pines furnish clear lumber of any required length or breadth, without a knot or blemish to mar their uniformity or beauty. Where some Indian fire has spread and struck a forest, so as to benumb its growth, the house builder finds his sound dry timber which readily takes the plane and a handsome finish, and the perfection of its seasoning in that dry atmosphere is a work of short duration.[11]

But other writers with extensive experience in the costs of transporting fuel, timber, and hay to Fort Philip Kearny when nearby supplies

[10] See lengthy testimony by numerous witnesses in "Proceedings of a Court of Inquiry re: the Fetterman Massacre," Special File GCMO–002236, Judge Advocate General's Records, NARS, RG 153; also, William B. Hazen, "Report of Inspection of Fort Philip Kearny, August 28th and 29th, 1866," to Adjutant General, Department of the Platte, August 29, 1866, NARS, RG 98, LR, Department of the Platte.

[11] Henry B. Carrington to Adjutant General, Department of the Platte, September 26, 1866, NARS, RG 98, LR, Department of the Platte; and Margaret Carrington, *Absaraka*, pp. 29, 162–163.

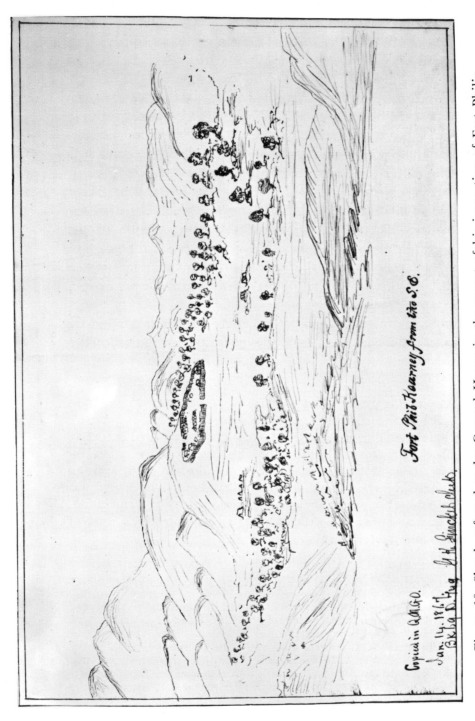

Figure 10. Sketch referred to by General Hazen in the report of his inspection of Fort Philip Kearny on August 29, 1866, probably by Ambrose G. Bierce, civilian topographic officer of the Hazen party. (*National Archives and Records Service.*)

became exhausted were not so enthusiastic about the location of the post.[12]

Carrington placed the stockade first in priority of construction, and started with an assortment of work details.[13] The men completed the northwest line of the stockade and part of the southeast line by August 9. Not satisfied with this rate of progress, Ten Eyck set up a new organization of the work as outlined on Figure 12.[14]

Logs of minimum one-foot thickness, slabbed to a four-inch touching surface on two sides, formed the walls of the stockade. They stood in a trench three feet deep, leaving their top eight feet exposed to form the wall. Some twenty-five hundred to three thousand such logs were in place by early September. The "blockhouses" (really artillery bastions) went into place on the west and east corners of the stockade on September 6, and gates were added shortly after.[15] Embrasures for small-arms fire, flared from six inches at their inner opening to about a foot at the outer face of the stockade, notched the top of the wall at about every fifth log joint (see Figure 13), and a continuous banquette three feet off the ground extended along each wall (Figure 13). Gates of heavy plank had smaller wicket gates through them.[16] Embrasures in the artillery bastions permitted the howitzers, if needed, to deliver an enfilading fire along the walls with canister.[17] The sentry stands in Carrington's time were open platforms, four by six feet, placed four feet off the ground in order to give a good view over the top of the stockade. They were probably located as shown on Figure 12.[18]

[12] Hazen, "Report of Inspection of Fort Philip Kearny, August 28th and 29th, 1866"; Colonel John E. Smith, 27th Infantry, to Adjutant General, Department of the Platte, July 18, 1867, NARS, RG 98, LR, Department of the Platte; Colonel John E. Smith, 27th Infantry, to Adjutant General, Department of the Platte, July 28, 1867, NARS, RG 98, LR, Department of the Platte; Major N. B. Sweitzer, 2nd Cavalry, "Report," November 15, 1867, dated at Philadelphia, Pennsylvania, to Adjutant General, Department of the Platte, NARS, RG 98, LR, Department of the Platte; Murphy, "Forgotten Battalion," p. 386.

[13] Hazen, "Report of Inspection of Fort Philip Kearny, August 28th and 29th, 1866"; Margaret Carrington, *Absaraka*, p. 121.

[14] General Order Number 11, Headquarters, Fort Philip Kearny, August 9, 1866, NARS, RG 98.

[15] *Ibid.*; General Order Number 14, Headquarters, Fort Philip Kearny, September 5, 1866, NARS, RG 98.

[16] Margaret Carrington, *Absaraka*, pp. 170–173.

[17] See Carrington's notes on sketch, Figure 15.

[18] F. M. Fessenden, "Personal Experiences in and Around Fort Phil Kearny," in Grace Raymond Hebard and E. A. Brininstool, *The Bozeman Trail* (Glendale, California: The Arthur H. Clark Co., 1960), II, 107; Special Order Number 37, Headquarters, Fort Philip Kearny, October 4, 1866, NARS, RG 98.

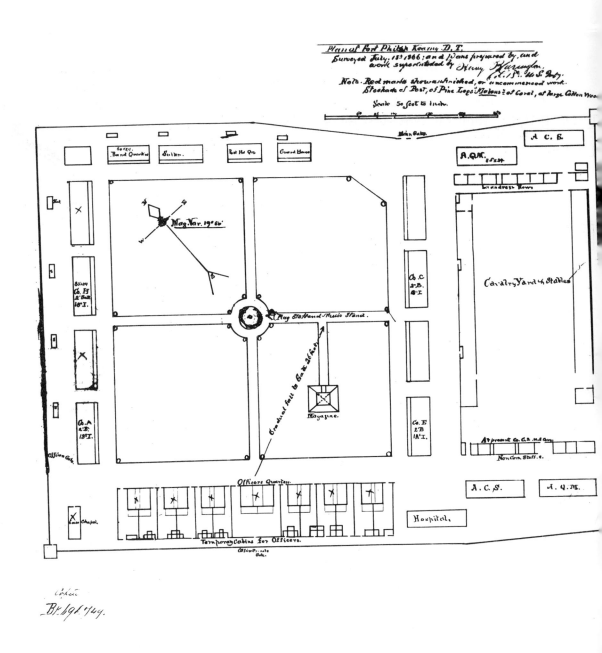

Figure 11. Carrington's last plan of Fort Philip Kearny during construction, with indications of the structures not yet built at the time he left. (*National Archives and Records Service.*)

34

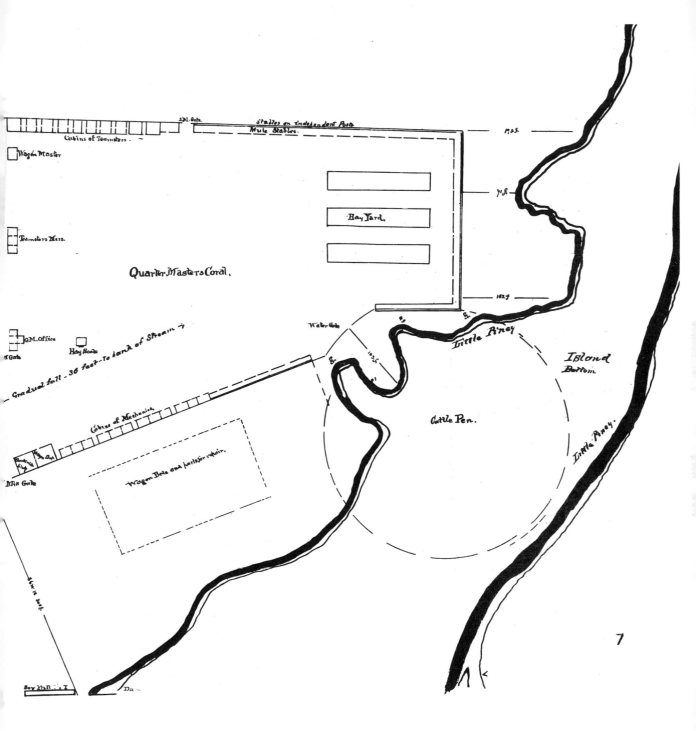

Cabins of Teamsters.

221 Gate.

Stables on independent Posts

Mule Stables.

r.s.s.

Wagon Master

y'.s.

Teamsters Mess.

Hay Yard.

Quarter Masters Coral.

102.s

Water Gate

Little Piney

Island
Bottom

Q.M. Office

Hay Scale

Gradual fall - 36 feet - To bank of Stream

Cabins of Mechanics.

Cattle Pen.

Little Piney.

Main Gate

Wagon Beds and harness repair.

7

Bar Scale - = I

Dam

35

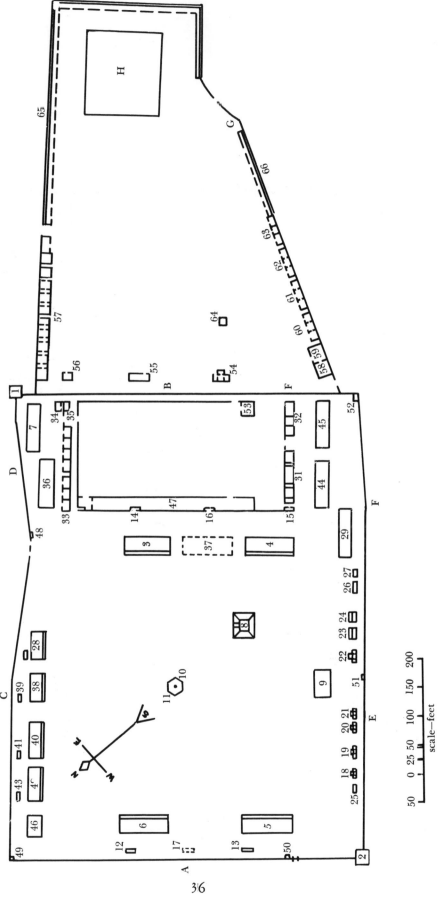

scale—feet

50   0 25 50   100   150   200

36

A and B. Segments of military stockade constructed by work details before August 9, 1866

C. Segment of stockade constructed by A Co., 2nd Bn., 18th Infantry, begun August 9, 1866, and completed before the end of August, 1866

D. Segment of stockade constructed by H Co., 2nd Bn., 18th Infantry, begun August 9, 1866, and completed before the end of August, 1866

E. Segment of stockade constructed by E Co., 2nd Bn., 18th Infantry, begun August 9, 1866, and completed before the end of August, 1866

F. Segment of stockade constructed by C Co., 2nd Bn., 18th Infantry, begun August 9, 1866, and completed before the end of August, 1866

G. Quartermaster's stockade, constructed by work details beginning September 25, 1866, apparently completed by November 10, 1866

H. Fence around hay yard, probably completed late in October, 1866

1. Blockhouse (referred to as the northeast blockhouse) built by Cos. A and H, 2nd Bn., 18th Infantry, September 6, 1866

2. Blockhouse (referred to as the southwest blockhouse) built by Cos. C and E, September 6, 1866

3 and 4. Barracks, roofed by the last week of September, 1866

5. Barracks, roofed by the last week of September, 1866. Men of this company installed a plank floor on their own time and with their own funds in the last week of October, 1866

6. Barracks, roofed by the last week of September, 1866

7. Commissary building (issue warehouse) roofed by the last week of September, 1866

8. Magazine, begun September 24, 1866, and completed October 10, 1866

9. Officers' quarters, single family, permanent, "approaching completion" by the end of September, although the interior was not completed by December 21, 1866

10. Flagstaff, begun October 11 and completed by the end of October

11. Music stand, begun October 11 and completed by the end of October

12–15. Company sinks, as provided for in General Order No. 24, October 18, 1866

16. Sink location, as provided for in General Order No. 24, October 18, 1866. Barracks under construction late in December, 1866; sink may or may not have been completed at that date

17. Sink location specified in General Order No. 24, October 18, 1866, but probably not begun before Carrington's departure

18–24. Temporary quarters for officers, begun under General Order No. 24, October 18, 1866

25–27. Structures of unknown function, possibly sinks for bachelor officers' quarters

28. Guardhouse, begun October 18, 1866

29. Temporary hospital, begun October 25, 1866

30. Sink for guardhouse

31 and 32. Non-commissioned officers' quarters, completed by November 12, 1866, and used in part as cavalry barracks pending completion of building No. 37

33. "Laundress row" apartment structure, completed by November 12, 1866

34 and 35. Probably non-commissioned officers' quarters, completed by November 12, 1866

36. Quartermaster's warehouse (issuing), completed before the end of 1866

37. Barracks, "well in progress" but not completed by December 21, 1866

38. Post headquarters building, "well in progress" but not completed by December 21, 1866

39. Sink, probably constructed during completion of work on the headquarters building, which it was intended to serve

40. Sutler's store, certainly completed by mid-December, 1866, and probably much earlier

41. Sink

42. Band headquarters, probably completed by the end of October, 1866

43. Sink, probably completed by the end of October, 1866

44. Commissary storehouse

45. Quartermaster's storehouse

46. Bakery

47. Cavalry stables

48–52. Locations of sentry stands on stockade

53. Related to incomplete stable to the north, possibly a tackroom or saddler's workshop

54. Quartermaster's office

55. Teamsters' mess

56. Wagonmaster (official?)

57. Civilian employees' quarters

58. Blacksmith shop

59. Wagon shop

60–63. "Cabins of mechanics"

64. Hay scale

65. Mule stable, extending around lower end of quartermaster's stockade

66. Probably an additional mule stable

Figure 12. An "as-built" plan of Fort Philip Kearny at the time of Carrington's departure, December, 1866, based on a detailed analysis of construction data from the post records of the fort and on Carrington's scaled drawings.

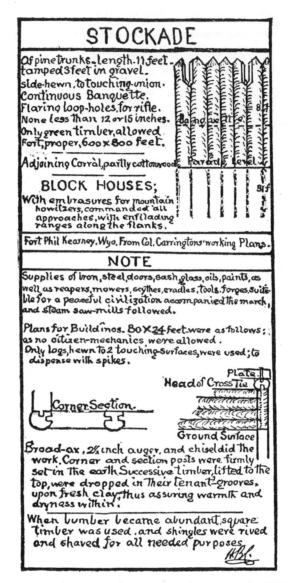

Figure 13. Carrington's sketch showing stockage and building construction detail. (*From Syrus T. Brady,* Indian Fights and Fighters.)

The completed main stockade gave the command a sense of security, for it could not be penetrated effectively by any weapon commonly used by the Indians, and its artillery could reach any substantial Indian force well out of small-arms range with an appropriate projectile. But perhaps this sense of security contributed to the lack of alertness on the part of the men and to the inattention of Carrington and many of his staff to matters of training and discipline.

Carrington drew up a plan for barracks (Figure 14), but changed it somewhat before beginning construction. He followed the plan structurally but shortened the buildings from 123 to 84 feet, mostly by omitting the kitchens and mess rooms.[19] He intended to add on the kitchens and mess rooms at the rear of each barracks,[20] but he did not accomplish this.[21] The barracks had dirt roofs: Private William Murphy, an enlisted man in the 18th Infantry, recalled that the "slabs from the mills were used in roofing the barracks and these were all covered with dirt."[22] Musician F. M. Fessenden described the log construction as in the Carrington sketches and said: "The roof was of poles about four inches thick, put close together, then covered with corn sacks or grass, with about six inches of earth over this for 'shingles.' Such a roof seldom leaked."[23] Only one barracks— that of Company A, 2nd Battalion, 18th Infantry—initially had a plank floor, and this was because the men hauled the logs themselves one Sunday late in October, 1866, and paid the sawyer's wages with money from their company fund.[24] Margaret Carrington states that the barracks had ten-foot ceilings.[25] If these were added after the peak of construction activity, they could have been made either of boards or of lath and plaster, since materials for both were available. These first four barracks went up rapidly, and were roofed around October 1,[26] and substantially completed by the end of that month.[27]

Construction of the commissary and quartermaster storehouses progressed at the same time as the barracks. These twenty-four-foot by eighty-four-foot buildings were of light framing, sided and roofed with one-inch boards and mill slabs.[28]

[19] Henry B. Carrington to Adjutant General, Department of the Platte, September 25, 1866, NARS, RG 98, LR, Department of the Platte.

[20] *Ibid.*

[21] Murphy, "Forgotten Battalion," p. 387; Major E. B. Grimes, "Report of Inspection of Fort Philip Kearny," NARS, RG 98, LR, Department of the Platte.

[22] Murphy, "Forgotten Battalion," p. 392.

[23] Fessenden, "Personal Experiences in and Around Fort Phil Kearny," p. 95.

[24] First Lieutenant George H. Palmer, Company A, 27th Infantry, to Post Adjutant, Fort Philip Kearny, January 22, 1868, NARS, RG 98, LR, Fort Philip Kearny.

[25] Margaret Carrington, *Absaraka*, p. 172.

[26] Henry B. Carrington to Adjutant General, Department of the Platte, September 25, 1866, NARS, RG 98, LR, Department of the Platte.

[27] Record of Events, Post Return for October, 1866, Fort Philip Kearny, NARS, RG 98.

[28] Grimes, "Report of Inspection of Fort Philip Kearny"; Henry B. Carrington to Adjutant General, Department of the Platte, September 25, 1866, NARS, RG 98, LR, Department of the Platte; Murphy, "Forgotten Battalion," p. 392.

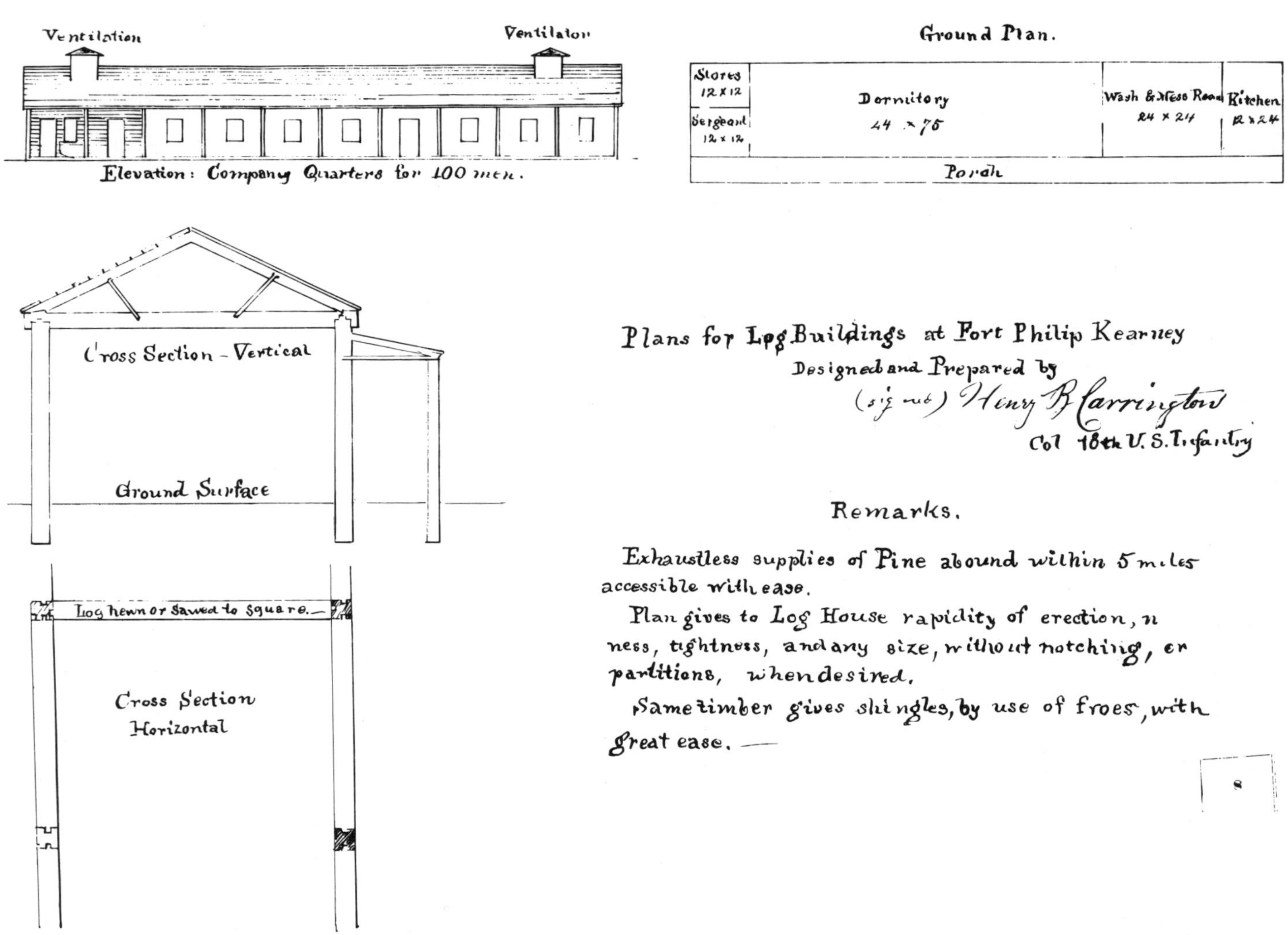

Ground Plan.

| Stores 12 x 12 Sergeant 12 x 12 | Dormitory 44 x 75 | Wash & Mess Room 24 x 24 | Kitchen 12 x 24 |

Porah

Ventilator.

Ventilation

Elevation: Company Quarters for 400 men.

Cross Section - Vertical

Ground Surface

Log hewn or sawed to square.

Cross Section Horizontal

Plans for Log Buildings at Fort Philip Kearney
Designed and Prepared by
(signed) Henry B. Carrington
Col 18th U.S. Infantry

Remarks.

Exhaustless supplies of Pine abound within 5 miles accessible with ease.

Plan gives to Log House rapidity of erection, neatness, tightness, and any size, without notching, or partitions, when desired.

Same timber gives shingles, by use of froes, with great ease. —

40

Figure 14. Carrington's original plan for barracks at Fort Philip Kearny, which he modified before construction by omitting the kitchen and shortening other areas, making the building eighty-four feet in length. (*National Archives and Records Service.*)

In September the shell of the large private quarters for the Carringtons was put up by members of the regimental band. This substantial frame house had siding of two-inch planks set on end and battened, a shingle roof, brick chimneys, and its ceilings and walls were lined with three-quarter-inch boards. The Carringtons moved in during October, but the interior was not completed until late December.[29]

Special work details built the magazine according to plan between September 24 and October 10.[30] (See Figure 15.)

Commissioned officers and their families lived in tents through the early autumn. Frances Courtney Grummond Carrington, Colonel Carrington's second wife, gives this description of their tent (occupied by herself and her husband at that time, Lieutenant G. W. Grummond):

> A detail of men from our company soon began operations. Two "A Tents," set up and drawn together, were soon in shape for our occupancy, the front of one for trunks, two rather dilapidated camp stools and a disfigured mess-chest, the other for two hospital bunks which filled nearly all the space, a small heating stove opposite, leaving a narrow passageway to a tarpaulin beyond, under which a cook-stove was placed ready for the preparation of the next morning's breakfast.[31]

The approach of winter made it necessary to build temporary huts for most of the officers. Frances Grummond Carrington describes her own new quarters with pleasure:

> The house was made of pine logs, recently felled and not quite dry, and small pine poles closely set for the best possible protection were covered with clay for the roof. Beneath were three—yes, actually three—rooms. I could hardly realize this luxury. In my haste to move I could not wait for any further drying process, but tacked blankets around the bed space and took the chances. Pieces of sheeting answered for window shades in two rooms and old newspapers, a very rare article covered the kitchen windows.

[29] Record of Events, Post Return for September, 1866, Fort Philip Kearny, NARS, RG 98; Frances Courtney Grummond Carrington, in *My Army Life* (New York: Lippincott, 1911), makes frequent mention of social functions held in this structure; Hazen, "Report of Inspection of Fort Philip Kearny, August 28th and 29th, 1866," states that the band members were mostly all on fatigue duty while building this house; Grimes, "Report of Inspection of Fort Philip Kearny," gives good measurements and descriptions of this structure, its condition, and additions made to it in 1867.

[30] Special Order Number 33, Headquarters, Fort Philip Kearny, September 24, 1866, NARS, RG 98; Special Order Number 43, Headquarters, Fort Philip Kearny, October 10, 1866, NARS, RG 98.

[31] Frances Carrington, *My Army Life,* pp. 101–102.

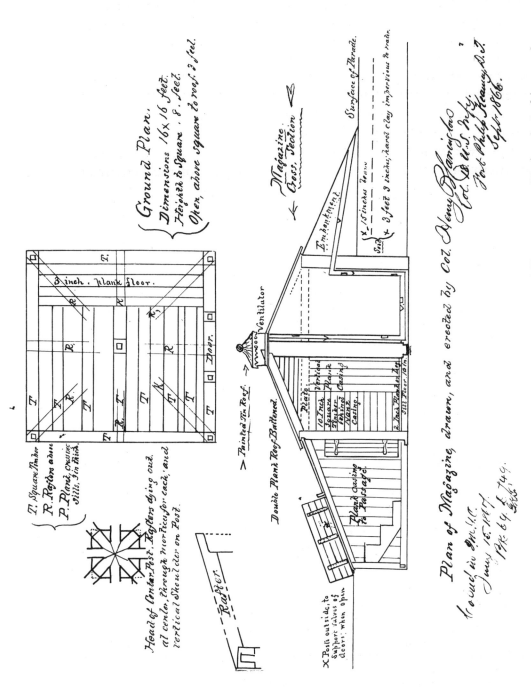

Figure 15. Carrington's plan for the magazine at Fort Philip Kearny. (National Archives and Records Service.)

The company tailor sewed gunny sacks from which the corn had been hurriedly emptied, and I soon had a carpet. My residence seemed palatial.[32]

The original hospital and the band quarters seem to have been built much like the barracks, of logs in panels. Laundresses' quarters, NCO's quarters, and citizen employees' quarters all appear to have been of temporary construction, much like the temporary officers' quarters in material. Stables were made of poles set in the ground "jacal" fashion, with pole and dirt roofs. Building No. 67 is almost certainly a quartermaster storage shed of similar construction. Workshops were similar jacal sheds. These buildings and the cottonwood quartermaster stockade were finished by the time of the Fetterman fight, and construction had begun on a headquarters' office and a fifth barracks. The post sutler's agent, John F. Kinney, built the only non-military structure inside the stockade in August, a twenty-four-foot by sixty-four-foot log structure.[33]

Carrington had to build extensively in order to get his sizable command under cover by winter. Reporting on his late August, 1866, inspection of the post, Hazen criticized the building of a stockade for a garrison of this size, for while he appreciated good design and construction, he clearly felt stockades were not essential. He forecast the resort to temporary construction of the crudest sort for many buildings, and felt that this would have been unnecessary if the stockade had been omitted.[34]

Less than three weeks before Carrington's departure, his new district quartermaster arrived—Captain (Brevet Brigadier General) George B. Dandy.[35] Dandy was a regular quartermaster officer with a fine talent for management, and he apparently did not get bogged down in day-to-day details. Dandy continued construction work through the winter as the weather allowed. During his tour at the post he built only nine completely new structures, but this number gives a deceptive view of his accomplishments, which in total upgraded the quality of the post considerably.[36] Dandy may have supervised completion of the headquarters' office, which Carrington had begun—a twenty-five-foot by fifty-foot frame building with one-inch board siding and a board roof.

[32] *Ibid.*, p. 104.

[33] Henry B. Carrington, description of events of December 21, 1866, in Senate Executive Document 33, 50th Cong., 1st Sess., p. 45.

[34] Hazen, "Report of Inspection of Fort Philip Kearny, August 28th and 29th, 1866."

[35] Record of Events, Post Return for December, 1866, Fort Philip Kearny, NARS, RG 98.

[36] Grimes, "Report of Inspection of Fort Philip Kearny."

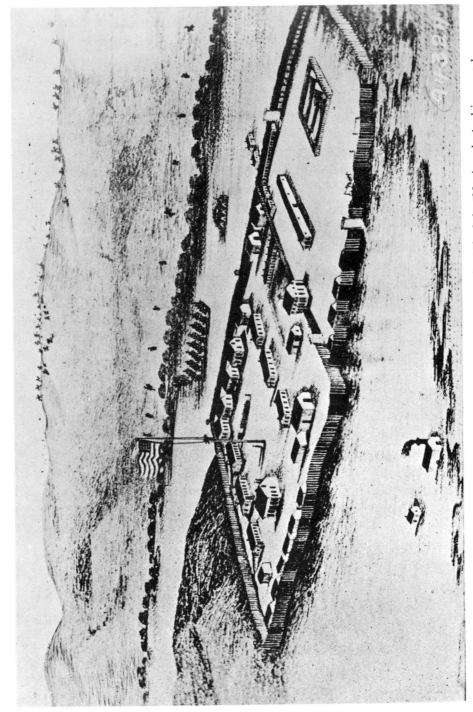

Figure 16. Sketch of Fort Philip Kearny by bugler Antonio Nicolai. (*National Archives and Records Service.*)

Dandy's first new construction was, naturally enough, a quartermaster's office, to replace the inadequate hut Captain F. H. Brown had used for this function. Selecting a site which was accessible to both units of the stockade, Dandy cut out a thirty-two-foot length of the wall dividing the stockade, and built his office there. Without doubt the best structure on the post, the office measured thirty-two by sixty-four feet, and was of good-quality frame construction. It stood fourteen feet from the ground to the top of its shingle roof, and was weather-boarded, lathed, and plastered.[37]

A. B. Ostrander, recently discharged from Fort Reno, arrived at Fort Philip Kearny on February 23, 1867, and found this building completed. An experienced clerk, Ostrander hired on as a civilian employee in the quartermaster's office, and worked in this building. The main floor contained a sizable outer room—Dandy's office—and a washroom. Ostrander was quartered in the loft, which was entered by a ladder in the washroom.[38] The floor of the office stood high enough to permit a good view from the windows, particularly to the east and northeast, where the ground sloped enough so that one could see over the stockade. An Anton Schonborn sketch (not shown), surviving only in copy form, appears to date from early spring, 1867. It shows the quartermaster's office completed, but the work on the new hospital not yet begun.[39]

If the June 23, 1867, date for the Nicolai sketch (Figure 16) is correct, then the quartermaster's office had been joined in Dandy's construction program by at least the shell of the new hospital. Built in response to requests from the post surgeon, Horton, and the medical director, Department of the Platte, the hospital was one of the post's largest buildings. L-shaped, each wing measured twenty-five feet in width, and the total length was 156 feet. It was situated near the northwest corner of the stockade, occupying the site of Carrington's bake house, and part of the Carrington-period band quarters, as well as some of the space once allotted for an additional barracks (Figure 16). The shell of the hospital was of log-in-panel construction similar to the barracks, chinked and lime-plastered, and had brick chimneys. The plastering was not finished until October, 1867,

[37] *Ibid.*

[38] A. B. Ostrander, *An Army Boy of the Sixties* (Chicago: World Book Company, 1926), pp. 196–198.

[39] *Ibid.*, pp. 198–199; see also Schonborn sketch accompanying Major David S. Gordon's reminiscent account, "The Relief of Fort Phil Kearny," which appears in *Journal of the Military Service Institute of the United States*, May, 1911.

probably because of the abundance of other construction work under way.[40]

Dandy built two log barracks. The first was a completion of the barracks for which Carrington was assembling materials on December 21 (Bldg. No. 37, Figure 12); the second was built directly across the parade ground from the first, between the two barracks built earlier on that side. Like the hospital, the barracks were of log-in-panel construction, chinked and lime-plastered, and had good shingle roofs, but they were smaller—twenty-six by one hundred feet. With a larger garrison squeezed within the confining walls of the Carrington stockade, Dandy cast about for a space saver, and found it by placing twenty-six-foot by forty-foot *basement kitchens* under the new barracks! This apparently worked well, for by Fall, 1867, he had remodeled all four of the early-period barracks to include these basement kitchens, also.[41]

Dandy also built a 32-foot by 160-foot quartermaster's storehouse, probably the long building extending across the quartermaster's corral, just below Dandy's office building. This was a frame structure with a shingle roof, sided with vertical, battened one-inch boards. (Ostrander noted that it had at least some civilian employee's bunks in it. The building may have been a temporary one, later torn down and replaced by the large storehouse, but this is conjectural.)[42]

A new commissary storehouse (precise location unknown) and a new guardhouse and a saddler's shop completed Dandy's new construction inside the stockade.[43]

The temporary cavalry stable of Carrington's time was torn down, and the horses were stabled in the old quartermaster's shed (Bldg. No. 67, Figure 12).[44]

Dandy certainly must have carried on extensive repairs and a general upgrading of all structures, for his work consumed over 600,000 board feet of lumber, over 250,000 shingles, 130,000 bricks,

[40] Post Surgeon's weekly report of December 8, 1866, NARS, RG 98, LR, Fort Philip Kearny; Communication Register and Endorsements, Fort Philip Kearny, February 12, 1867, entry of Department Medical Director's and Surgeon General's comments on above report, NARS, RG 98; Grimes, "Report of Inspection of Fort Philip Kearny"; Special Order Number 175, Headquarters, Fort Philip Kearny, October 11, 1867, NARS, RG 98.
[41] Grimes, "Report of Inspection of Fort Philip Kearny."
[42] *Ibid.*
[43] *Ibid.*
[44] *Ibid.*; see also Figures 17 and 18.

and considerable lath—all made at the post—plus 38 panel doors and 250 new window sashes, which arrived in the fall of 1867.[45]

Outside the Fort Philip Kearny stockade were a number of related structures. Carrington's first steam sawmill arrived at the fort in August, 1866, and another came by October.[46] The saw frame from one such mill survives at the fort today. These mills were housed in slab-covered frame buildings as shown on Figures 16 and 17.[47] One of these mills burned down on the night of June 19, 1867.[48] A water-powered (turbine-driven) mill replaced it that fall, housed in a building of similar construction.[49] Carrington's plan (Figure 11) shows a dam on the Little Piney that was used to store boiler water for the steam sawmills. An injection pump intake pipe is still in place in the stream bank at this point.

Pickets were stationed regularly on the nearest high points—Sullivant Hill and Pilot Hill. The latter station was the most frequently used, and here troops built a platform, protected on its south approach by an entrenchment of some sort.[50]

Timber-cutting parties built three blockhouses in the Pinery in the late summer or early fall of 1866.[51] A surviving Carrington map locates these structures, along with the wagon bridge built by Carrington on December 20, 1866. This bridge, built of three-inch planks, supported by log stringers, was sixteen feet wide and forty-five feet long.[52] It remained in use for some time. Lieutenant Alexander Wishart crossed it with a cavalry column at the time of high water on July 18, 1867.[53]

[45] *Ibid.*; Report of Board of Survey, November 7, 1867, NARS, RG 98, LR, Fort Philip Kearny.

[46] Record of Events, Post Return for August, 1866, Fort Philip Kearny, NARS, RG 98; Fessenden, "Personal Experiences in and Around Fort Phil Kearny," p. 92; Special Order Number 48, Headquarters, Fort Philip Kearny, October 18, 1866, NARS, RG 98; Special Order Number 52, Headquarters, Fort Philip Kearny, October 23, 1866, NARS, RG 98.

[47] Grimes, "Report of Inspection of Fort Philip Kearny."

[48] Report of a Board of Officers convened under Special Order Number 98, June 20, 1867, NARS, RG 98, LR, Fort Philip Kearny.

[49] Report of a Board of Survey, November 7, 1867, at Fort Philip Kearny, NARS, RG 98, LR, Fort Philip Kearny; Grimes, "Report of Inspection of Fort Philip Kearny."

[50] Max Littman, "The Wagon Box Fight as I Saw It," in Hebard and Brininstool, *The Bozeman Trail*, II, 81.

[51] Margaret Carrington, *Absaraka*, pp. 148, 161.

[52] Henry B. Carrington, statement in Senate Executive Document 33, 50th Cong., 1st Sess., p. 39.

[53] Alexander Wishart, First Lieutenant, 27th Infantry, "Diary for 1867," copy of an original (Glenn D. Sweem collection, Sheridan, Wyoming), July 18, 1867. (Hereinafter cited as Wishart, "Diary.")

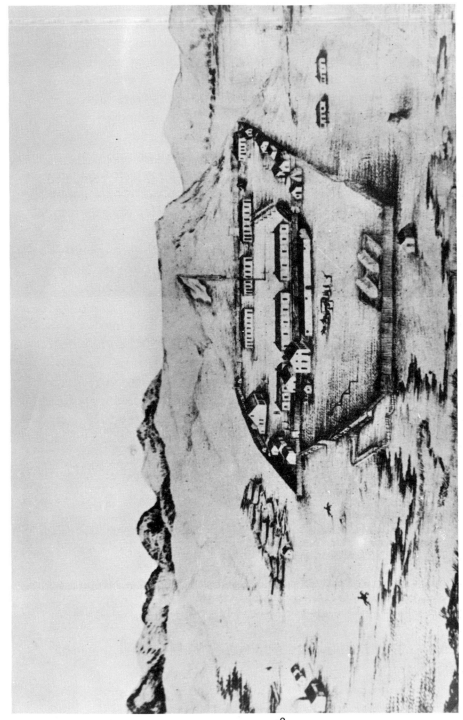

Figure 17. Fort Philip Kearny, from a sketch made by a sergeant of the 27th Infantry in 1867. *(Henry B. Freeman Collection, Wyoming State Archives and Historical Department.)*

48

Throughout the spring and summer of 1867, there was considerable Indian Peace Commission activity around Fort Philip Kearny. William Murphy states that the commissioners had a log cabin built as an office and warehouse, "about 300 yards from the fort and on the banks of the Big Piney, and also a foot bridge for the Indians to cross."[54]

In addition, civilians built a number of cabins near the fort. James Wheatly built the first one, with Ten Eyck's permission, in September, 1866. Here his wife ran an eating house for civilians.[55] Wheatly died with the Fetterman party in December, 1866, but his wife remained at the post, operating the establishment. She married a civilian wheelwright for the army, George Breckenridge, on June 3, 1868, and together they continued to operate the restaurant until the post was abandoned.[56] Mr. and Mrs. Charles Washington had an "eating house" about a hundred yards from the stockade from 1867 to 1868, when the post was abandoned. Walter J. Harden and F. J. Fairbrast kept a "ranche" and billiard room near the post until just before the end of occupancy in 1868.[57] John S. Morris, "ranche keeper," apparently operated only in the spring of 1868, and left on June 7.[58]

During its tenure, Fort Philip Kearny was refined and improved largely by George B. Dandy, Acting Quartermaster. The changes he made testify to his vision, energy, and ability. Nevertheless, the fort remained within the bounds of the Carrington-period fortifications, for better or worse. The commanding officer's quarters and the four original barracks dominate the scene, backed by the cramped hovels of laundresses and NCO's, also of Carrington's making. Thus, to the casual observer Fort Philip Kearny will probably remain very much "Carrington's Fort," although he was there for scarcely more than a quarter of its duration as an active post.

[54] Murphy, "Forgotten Battalion," pp. 395–397.
[55] James Wheatly to Post Commander, Fort Philip Kearny, August 30, 1866, NARS, RG 98, LR, Fort Philip Kearny; Special Order Number 17, August 31, 1866, Headquarters, Fort Philip Kearny, NARS, RG 98.
[56] Murphy, "Forgotten Battalion," p. 401.
[57] "List of Citizens at Post, and How Employed," Fort Philip Kearny, 1st and 2nd quarters of 1868, NARS, RG 98, LR, Fort Philip Kearny. This is a logbook-type listing with weekly checks of citizens at the post, through the quarter, with many notes on arrivals and departures.
[58] *Ibid.*

Chapter 4.   Resources of the Early Posts

ORGANIZATION, 1865–1868

The initial garrison at Fort Connor (Fort Reno) consisted of six companies of the 6th Michigan Volunteer Cavalry which were quickly replaced by Companies C and D, 5th U.S. Volunteers, supplemented by Company A, Omaha Scouts.[1] This force was directly responsible to General P. E. Connor, Commanding General, District of the Plains. Late in August, 1865, orders from the Military Division of the Missouri dissolved Connor's command, but word of the change did not reach the Powder River country for another month. After that time, the post commander reported directly to Headquarters, U.S. Forces, Kansas and the Territories, until a spring reorganization brought the post under Headquarters, Department of the Platte, newly established in Omaha.[2]

When Carrington reached the Powder River country late in June, 1866, he organized the Mountain District, which included the territory north of the North Platte River, along the "Montana Road," to Virginia City. Generally, however, Bozeman Pass marked the northwestern limit of Mountain District activities.[3]

Fort Reno continued as an active post in the Mountain District, and the Carrington column established Fort Philip Kearny and Fort C. F. Smith. As commanding officer of the Mountain District, Carrington issued orders directly to the post commanders.

[1] Leroy R. Hafen and Ann W. Hafen, editors, *The Powder River Campaigns and Sawyer's Expedition, 1865* (Glendale, California: The Arthur H. Clark Co., 1961), pp. 1–59.

[2] G. M. Dodge, "Report," U.S. Forces, Kansas and the Territories, November 1, 1865, *War of the Rebellion*, Ser. I, XLVIII, Pt. 1, 335–348.

[3] Henry B. Carrington, statement in Senate Executive Document 33, 50th Congress, 1st Session, p. 2.

In September, 1866, orders were given to dissolve the Mountain District and make the post commanders directly responsible to Department Headquarters in Omaha. These orders reached the Mountain District on October 13.[4] Carrington personally assumed command of Fort Philip Kearny on October 7, 1866,[5] and retained that command until relieved by the arrival of Lieutenant Colonel Henry W. Wessells on January 18, 1867.[6] Then, orders from the Department of the Platte reactivated the Mountain District on January 1, 1867, and it remained active until the end of July, 1868.

During this period, there was a reorganization of some units in the regulars. The 1866 Army Bill provided for the expansion of the number of infantry regiments by taking the second and third battalions of the Civil War three-battalion regiments and activating each as a full regiment. This change, made effective on January 1, 1867, left the 1st Battalion, 18th Infantry, as simply the 18th Infantry; the 2nd Battalion became the new 27th Infantry; and the 3rd Battalion became the new 36th Infantry. Each of these units was then organized along the lines established for standardized infantry regiments.[7]

The tables of garrison strengths, Appendix A, show the distribution of organizational elements and their strengths for the period.

MILITARY PERSONNEL

Companies C and D, 5th U.S. Volunteers, which garrisoned Fort Reno, comprised one of the last Civil War units to be mustered out. The two companies were composed largely of inmates recruited from Union prison camps for service in the West. Their officers were men who had missed appointments to better commands at the close of the war. The primary aim of both officers and enlisted personnel alike seemed to be merely to survive until their eventual mustering out. They were perhaps an adequate but certainly not a choice force to

[4] *Ibid.,* p. 32.

[5] General Orders, Number 21 and Number 22, Headquarters, Fort Philip Kearny, October 7, 1866, NARS, RG 98.

[6] General Orders, Number 3 and Number 4, Headquarters, Fort Philip Kearny, January 18, 1867, NARS, RG 98.

[7] A good discussion of this reorganization is available in the booklet by A. B. Ostrander, *The Bozeman Trail Forts Under General Philip St. George Cooke* (privately printed, Seattle, Wash.: December, 1932). Orders and correspondence of the Department of the Platte confirm Ostrander's outline of the reorganization and the subsequent personnel changes.

garrison Fort Reno through the holding action of late 1865 and early 1866.[8]

Company A, Omaha Scouts, was actually composed of Winnebago Indians, who had been removed from Minnesota to Fort Thompson, Dakota, then moved again to share a reservation with the Omahas in northeastern Nebraska. Without land, capital, or opportunities for employment, these Indians had little to lose, and at least some prospect of gain, by their stay at Fort Reno.

The regulars of the 2nd Battalion, 18th Infantry, who came into the Powder River country in 1866, were a diverse lot. Each company had at least a few men with Civil War experience, and many had served with the regiment throughout the war; however, most of the men were recent recruits. Those who arrived at Fort Reno were of reasonably good character,[9] their less hardy and more transient comrades having deserted on the long up-country march. Over one hundred and fifty men deserted from the regiment between Fort Leavenworth and Fort Sedgwick. Thus, the ones who arrived with Carrington were tough and willing workers, but they lacked training and there was little provision for it in the summer and fall of 1866.

Most of the commissioned officers of the 18th Infantry, the 27th Infantry, and the 2nd Cavalry serving at Fort Reno and Fort Philip Kearny through late 1866 and early 1867 had had some Civil War service; but age, old wounds, disease, and personality disorders limited the effectiveness of many of them. For the more competent, opportunities in civilian life held a strong lure. Of the sixty commissioned officers who actually served at Fort Philip Kearny between July, 1866, and July, 1868, only thirty-six remained in the army after January 1, 1871. Four were killed in action, several died on active duty, and nineteen left because of retirement, resignation, or dismissal in that three-and-one-half-year period. This rapid turnover, combined with reorganization, contributed to momentary inefficiency in the units, but the quality of officers steadily improved during 1867 and 1868 at these posts.[10]

[8] Muster Rolls, Companies C and D, 5th U.S. Volunteers, NARS, RG 94; also, the excellent discussion in D. Alexander Brown, *The Galvanized Yankees* (Urbana, Ill.: The University of Illinois Press, 1963).

[9] Muster Rolls, 18th U.S. Infantry, NARS, RG 94; see also, Carrington's many comments on the hard work and long hours willingly put in by these men.

[10] Record of Events, Post Returns, July, 1866—July, 1867, Fort Philip Kearny, NARS, RG 98. Service data from Francis B. Heitman, *Historical Register and Dictionary of the United States Army, 1789–1903* (Washington: Government Printing Office, 1903).

GOVERNMENT CIVILIAN EMPLOYEES

The most unappreciated personnel component at the western army posts were the civilian employees of the government. They ranged from laborers, teamsters, and skilled tradesmen to the highly paid clerks, interpreters, and guides. Through the peak of activity at Fort Philip Kearny, when it served as Mountain District headquarters, there were about a hundred persons on the quartermaster's civilian payroll, with 171 positions on the list for October, 1867. These citizen employees were clearly a manpower resource not to be overlooked in any discussion of the early posts. They included young people fresh from the states, working their way to the mining country, as well as seasoned westerners left over from fur-trading days. Such frontier notables as Jim Bridger, James P. Beckwourth, Jack Stead, Rafael Gallegos, and Mich Bouyer were on the Fort Philip Kearny payrolls at one time or another.[11]

Ostrander comments favorably on the teamsters and clerks he knew:

> It is high time that these men who often bore the brunt of things were given open and adequate praise. On the trail, when there were indications of an actual attack or a genuine battle with Indians, the packers and teamsters had to make the corral and keep control of their stock. Any undue excitement on their part might result in stampeding a whole outfit; and a stampede under such conditions was fully as disastrous as a successful charge of wild Indians. It was a post full of danger, requiring a cool head and a steady hand. On the work of the teamsters when the outfit was under fire, the success of the whole command depended. These packers, teamsters, and wagon bosses may have been considered as tough characters. They probably thought they had to be, for theirs was a rough job. Many of them were hard drinkers, hard swearers, and addicted to vices; but they generally proved true blue whenever tight pinches came.[12]
>
> . . . .
>
> I saw some familiar faces. Two clerks who had occupied quarters near mine in Fort Laramie were there. They were both first-class accountants and could get away with more work in three hours than ordinary clerks would in three days.[13]

[11] Citizen employees are listed in the post returns only by job title and pay—in essence, a list of positions filled and money paid out. For some months, rosters of all civilians at the post are available in the Post Adjutant's letterbooks.

[12] A. B. Ostrander, *An Army Boy of the Sixties* (Chicago: World Book Company, 1926), p. 188.

[13] *Ibid.,* p. 196.

CONTRACTORS' EMPLOYEES

There were substantial numbers of civilian contractors in the Powder River country. With its small garrison, Fort Reno usually had few such employees, and they were hired for a very short work season; but as Mountain District headquarters, Fort Philip Kearny employed large numbers of contractor personnel throughout much of the year. Detailed data are available for some months, while for others there is only scanty information. It is clear, though, that except for midwinter there were usually several dozen contractor employees at any one time at Fort Philip Kearny.

These men were as diverse a group as the government civilian employees. They worked for the contractors when jobs were available, then for the quartermaster after contracts were fulfilled, and some perhaps hunted or lived on their savings until work opened up in the spring. With such seasonal shifts in employment, there were usually a number of men between jobs at the post. Together with discharged soldiers and other men awaiting the movement of wagon trains up or down the trail, they brought the unemployed community at Fort Philip Kearny to twenty or more.[14] The records show frequent changes in their status. Discharged soldiers sometimes went to work as government civilian employees, and government civilian employees often worked for contractors. Men quitting passing wagon trains found employment in either capacity, and were themselves usually replaced by men earning their transportation up or down the trail. In one case a discharged teamster from a passing wagon train even enlisted as a soldier in the 27th Infantry.

William Bailey's mining party of about forty men arrived at Fort Philip Kearny in September, 1866.[15] They were first employed to guard contract hay cutters.[16] Later they shifted from one job to another individually. Bailey, Van Valzah, and John Phillips all worked as mail carriers for varying periods of time. Phillips also worked for a contractor and for the quartermaster.[17]

[14] "List of citizens at the post and how employed," in the Post Adjutant's letterbooks, NARS, RG 98. Lists are available for the first and second quarters of 1868, plus that portion of the third quarter preceding abandonment.

[15] Henry B. Carrington to Adjutant General, Department of the Platte, September 25, 1866, NARS, RG 98, LR, Department of the Platte.

[16] John Bratt, *Trails of Yesterday* (Chicago: University Publishing Co., 1921), pp. 90–91.

[17] "List of citizens and how employed"; see also, comments on citizen employees in Murphy, Ostrander, and other reminiscent accounts.

OTHER CIVILIANS

The exact business relationships at the sutler's store at Fort Philip Kearny are somewhat obscure. Margaret Carrington and others refer to John Fitch Kinney as the business representative of A. J. Bottsford, Sutler.[18] More casual writers often refer to Kinney as the sutler. The post records usually refer to Kinney as a clerk, with J. B. Weston or Joseph Saunders signing correspondence and documents for the Bottsford firm. Hazen clarifies this somewhat, stating that Bottsford had not been at the fort since his appointment by the Secretary of War, and that Kinney arrived in August, 1866, with a power-of-attorney to handle Bottsford's business at the store. Kinney bought out the stock of J. W. Hugus (who accompanied the Carrington column). Hazen states that Kinney had sixty thousand dollars invested in the business at the time of Hazen's inspection in August, 1866.[19] The 1866 Army Bill abolished post sutlerships as of July 1, 1867, and authorized the Acting Commissary of Subsistence at each post to carry sutler's goods. Saunders, addressed as "sutler-in-charge," received notice of this in February, 1867.[20] On July 1, 1867, Brevet Brigadier General Henry W. Wessells granted special permission to Kinney to carry on his business at the sutler's store.[21] William Murphy believed that some form of partnership existed between Kinney, Coe, Carter, and others.[22] Prevailing business practices throughout the West in this period make this seem entirely probable. W. B. Hugus appears in the records as post trader in April, 1868, under a new system of appointments, and he continued in this capacity until the abandonment of the post.[23] The post trader usually had a small number of employees.

Fort Reno's first sutler was A. S. Leighton. He came into the Powder River country with Connor's column, and held the

---

[18] Margaret I. Carrington, *Absaraka, Home of the Crows* (Chicago: Lakeside Press, 1950), p. 164.

[19] William B. Hazen, "Report of Inspection of Fort Philip Kearny, August 28th and 29th, 1866," to Adjutant General, Department of the Platte, August 29, 1866, NARS, RG 98, LR, Department of the Platte; J. B. Weston to Post Adjutant, Fort Philip Kearny, December 14, 1866, NARS, RG 98, LR, Fort Philip Kearny.

[20] General Order Number 6, Adjutant General's Office, January 26, 1867, forwarded to Saunders on February 26, 1867, endorsed by Post Adjutant, NARS, RG 98, LR, Fort Philip Kearny.

[21] General Order Number 45, Headquarters, Fort Philip Kearny, July 1, 1867, NARS, RG 98.

[22] William Murphy, "The Forgotten Battalion," *Annals of Wyoming*, VII, Number 2 (October 1930), 385.

[23] "List of citizens and how employed," second quarter, 1868.

appointment by authority of Connor and General Pope.[24] Finn G. Burnett stated that a friend of his, Kemp Caldwell, actually ran the store throughout much of the post's occupancy.[25]

DEPENDENTS

The isolation of the early posts deterred many men from taking their families to the Powder River country, and few indeed came after hostilities with the Indians had begun. The following list, compiled by a thorough screening of all available sources, is as complete as possible:

Margaret Carrington, wife of Colonel Henry B. Carrington
James Carrington, son   „   „   „   „   „
Harry Carrington, son   „   „   „   „   „
"Black George," servant   „   „   „   „   „
Wife of Doctor Samuel Horton, Post Surgeon
Frances Grummond, wife of Lieutenant G. W. Grummond (later married Colonel Henry B. Carrington)
Wife of Lieutenant Wands
Robert Wands, son of Lieutenant Wands
Colored maid of Mrs. Wands
Wife of Bandmaster Curry
Two sons of   „   „
Wife of Private John Murray, a hospital cook, Company A, 2nd Battalion, 18th Infantry (Mrs. Murray ran a boarding house for teamsters.)
Belle Murray, daughter of Private John Murray (Belle Murray was for a time a hospital matron.)
Wife of Private Andrew Hannibal, a hospital attendant, Company E, 27th Infantry (Mrs. Hannibal worked for a time as a hospital matron.)
Three daughters of Private Andrew Hannibal
Wife of John Maurer
Wife of a man named Laughlotts
Daughter of Laughlotts
Wife of Lieutenant Bisbee
Jean Bisbee, daughter of Lieutenant Bisbee

[24] Henry B. Carrington to Adjutant General, Department of the Platte, July 1, 1866, NARS, RG 98; Hazen, "Report of Inspection of Fort Philip Kearny."
[25] F. G. Burnett, "Fort C.F. Smith and the Hayfield Fight," in Grace Raymond Hebard and E. A. Brininstool, *The Bozeman Trail* (Glendale, California: The Arthur H. Clark Co., 1960), II, 171.

Wife of Musician F. M. Fessenden
Daughter of „   „ „   „
Colored maid of Captain Ten Eyck

Wives of enlisted men, employed as hospital matrons for varying periods of time, were:

Mrs. Samuel Carey
Mrs. McGuinn
Mrs. Richard Keogh
Mrs. Michael Ratchford

As the Indian scare subsided, at least two officers brought their dependents to live at Fort Philip Kearny:

Wife of Brevet Major (Captain) D. S. Gordon, 2nd Cavalry
Two sons of   „   „   „ „   „   „   „
Wife of Lieutenant C. H. Warrens

Army Regulations (128, R.A.R.) authorized four laundresses per company, but this level may never have been reached at Fort Philip Kearny. Hazen noted that there were four laundresses there in August, 1866. These jobs were usually filled by the wives of enlisted men, but occasionally a single girl took such an appointment. One, the notorious "Colored Susan" of Company H, 2nd Battalion, caused quite a stir in the garrison in 1866:

> I. A laundress of Co. H. (Colored Susan), having been reputed for selling ardent spirits to soldiers and it being known that she makes and sells at exhorbitant [*sic*] rates pies made of government flour and fruit, the commanding officer of said company will examine and report whether said pies are made from surplus savings of the company and with their consent, and whether if not made from her own ration, the profits enure to the benefit of the company.
>
> II. The company commander is also advised for his information that the same woman is disorderly, breeding mischief in the garrison by inciting officers' servants to abandon their situations, and as an inducement setting forth the large sums of money she realizes and accumulates by the methods above referred to.
>
> This woman, profane, abusive and of bad repute before her arrival, must observe better behavior or she will not be tolerated in the garrison.[26]

[26] Data on dependents from Margaret I. Carrington, *Absaraka*; Frances Courtney Grummond Carrington, *My Army Life* (New York: Lippincott, 1911); F. M. Fessenden, "Personal Experiences in and around Fort Phil Kearny," in Hebard and Brininstool, *Bozeman Trail*; Wishart "Diary"; scattered incidental references in orders and correspondence; "Colored Susan" is mentioned in Special Order Number 75, Fort Philip Kearny, November 24, 1866, NARS, RG 98.

Additional dependants at Fort Philip Kearny included the wife of James Wheatly and their two sons, the wife of Charles Washington, possibly the Cheyenne wife of Jack Stead, and, for several months, the widow of Trader Gasseau.

Hazen reported no laundresses at Fort Reno. Grimes, in his inventory of structures, lists no laundresses' quarters, although reminiscent accounts identify one such building (see Chapter 2). There are no records of dependents at Fort Reno.

TRANSPORT

The biggest and costliest problem in establishing and operating the early posts was transportation. When the posts beyond Fort Reno were in the planning stages, primary supply points for the Powder River region were Fort Leavenworth and the town of Omaha. The closest of these—Omaha—was more than 650 miles from Fort Reno, over wagon trails that were unimproved except for bridges over a few secondary streams east of Grand Island on the Platte. Distances such as these required a large expenditure of man hours, stock, and forage, so transportation charges were high by necessity. In early 1866, contractors charged $1.79 per hundred pounds per hundred miles to other High Plains posts.[27] Adding to this the cost of rail or water transport from the point of origin brought the total shipping costs even higher.

Hazen, with a sharp eye for logistic problems, saw that the high overland shipping costs were a major problem for the Bozeman Trail posts. He recognized the trail for what it was—a temporary emigrant route, unsuitable for transporting army supplies. In its stead, he proposed an overland wagon road direct from the Missouri River at the mouth of the Musselshell to Fort C. F. Smith, thus cutting high-cost wagon shipment to a minimum mileage. Hazen also brought out the fact that in-transit loss and damage averaged about one-tenth less by steamboat than by wagon. His suggestion was not adopted, however, but one post, Fort C. F. Smith, did have fair sources of supply for some commodities in the Gallatin Valley, and was usually better supplied than the other Powder River posts.[28]

[27] Raymond W. Welty, "Supplying the Frontier Military Posts," *Kansas Historical Quarterly*, VII, Number 2 (May 1938), 156; Hazen's reports also contain much information on transportation.

[28] Special Order Number 38, Headquarters, Fort Philip Kearny, October 5, 1866, NARS, RG 98.

Transportation costs dropped steadily in 1866 and 1867 as the Union Pacific pushed westward at a rate of more than a mile a day. By October, 1866, two trainfuls of supplies reached Fort Philip Kearny, having loaded up at Lone Tree Station (now Central City), Nebraska Territory. A year later, Wells Fargo contract trains loaded Powder River supplies at Julesburg, Colorado Territory, and at Cheyenne.[29]

Nevertheless, the costs of delivered supplies still remained high, even with the shorter haul. Commissary supplies sold to contractors and their employees at cost-plus-transportation in the fall of 1867 included: flour, $31\frac{1}{2}$¢ per pound; sugar, $28\frac{1}{4}$¢ per pound; coffee, 34¢ per pound; and salt, $14\frac{1}{2}$¢ per pound.[30] Contract trains from Cheyenne took from eleven to thirty days to reach Fort Philip Kearny.[31] Such cost and time factors had much to do with the army's steady effort to abandon the small, isolated posts and develop strong bases for more mobile forces located on good transportation lines, such as the railroads and the navigable rivers.[32]

Food

The daily ration for each man during the years 1865–1868 consisted of:

> . . . three-fourths of a pound of pork or bacon, or one and a fourth pound of fresh or salt beef; eighteen ounces of bread or flour, or twelve ounces of hard bread, or one and a fourth pound corn meal; and *at the rate to one hundred rations* of eight quarts of beans, or in lieu thereof ten pounds of rice, or in lieu thereof twice per week one hundred and fifty ounces of desiccated potatoes, and one hundred ounces of mixed vegetables; ten pounds of coffee, or in lieu thereof one and one half pound of tea; fifteen pounds of sugar; four quarts of vinegar; . . .[33] [emphasis supplied].

This was plain fare at its best, and the best did not become available until mid-1867 at the Powder River posts. Large-scale operations on

[29] Deposition by Wagonmaster William McPherson, given at Fort Philip Kearny, December 8, 1867, NARS, RG 98, LR, Fort Philip Kearny.

[30] Copy of the receipted account of J. R. Porter with the Acting Commissary of Subsistence, Fort Philip Kearny, September and October, 1867, NARS, RG 98, LR, Fort Philip Kearny.

[31] Wagon Train Book for 1868, Fort Philip Kearny, NARS, RG 98.

[32] Robert W. Frazer, *Forts of the West* (Norman: University of Oklahoma Press, 1965), p. xvi.

[33] 1191, Revised Army Regulations, Adjutant General's Office (Washington, D.C.: 1861 edition).

the Plains necessitated the stockpiling of supplies at nearly all posts. As volunteer units moved down the trails for mustering out in the fall of 1865, their surplus supplies were left behind with the post quartermasters. A year's rations for five hundred men were stored at Fort Connor.[34] But spoilage, issues to Indians, and irregularities in the records at many posts resulted in smaller real stores than were carried on the records in faraway St. Louis.[35] It seems safe also to assume that isolated garrisons like that of Fort Reno used up the best-quality supplies of those large quantities stored there. The composition of Fort Reno's garrison virtually assures that this must have been the case.

Carrington wrote from Fort Reno on his arrival:

> . . . In nearly all respects I find that I did not err in anticipating deficiencies and indifferent quality of supplies en route. I was unable to draw sufficient hard bread to last from post to post. Much that was procured was musty. Flour drawn at Laramie was musty, caked and very poor, to a considerable extent, with no supply of baking utensils.[36]

The Carrington column stayed over a few days at Fort Reno, loading some of their supply wagons. Private William Murphy, who was detailed to this work, wrote:

> We loaded up some sacks of bacon. I do not know how old it was, but the fat had commenced to sluff off from the lean and it was from three to five inches thick. There was a lot of flour in the store rooms and the mice had tunneled through it and the bacon, evidently for some time.[37]

Such, then, were the reserves of rations at Fort Reno and at Fort Philip Kearny for the fall and winter of 1866–1867. The garrisons did not get down to these stores for some time. Private A. B. Ostrander, the headquarters clerk at Fort Reno late in 1866, described his first meal at the post, a soup made of dried vegetables: "Right here I shall add that while the desiccated vegetables lasted we enjoyed pretty good health. . . ."[38] Fort Reno's supply of vegetables lasted until late January.[39]

[34] *War of the Rebellion*, Series I, XLVIII, Part 1, Appendix M, 365.

[35] These topics are frequently mentioned in the correspondence of Fort Laramie for this period.

[36] Henry B. Carrington, at Fort Reno, to Adjutant General, Department of the Platte, July 1, 1866, NARS, RG 98, LR, Department of the Platte.

[37] Murphy, "Forgotten Battalion," pp. 384–385.

[38] Ostrander, *An Army Boy of the Sixties*, p. 150.

[39] Special Order Number 9, Headquarters, Fort Reno, January 30, 1867, NARS, RG 98.

Fort Philip Kearny's garrison fared somewhat better at the beginning, but suffered more than the men at Fort Reno that winter. Some officers and their families arrived at Fort Philip Kearny with dairy cattle, poultry, pigs, and private stocks of rations to supplement the standard items available from the Commissary of Subsistence.[40] Even some of the enlisted men had dairy cattle.[41]

With reasonably good pay and well-stocked sutler's shelves, hardship seemed far away to these officers and their families enjoying a picnic on the Piney one summer day in 1866:

> . . . elk steaks . . . canned lobster, cove oysters, and salmon were a very fair first course; and associated with the game, were jellies, pineapples, tomatoes, sweet corn, peas, pickles and such creature comforts, while puddings, pies and domestic cake, from doughnuts and gingerbread up to plum cake and jelly cake, with coffee, and Madam Cliquot for those who wished it, and pipes and cigars for the gentlemen. . . .[42]

But conditions changed rapidly that fall. Wolves caught the turkeys, the chickens died, and Indians ran off the larger stock.[43] Herds of beef cattle could not be taken to pasture for lack of adequate defenses, and by mid-October they were eating hay intended for winter use. The situation worsened when troop re-enforcements arrived in January, 1867, for they brought no rations with them.[44] For two months supplies were low, and even conservative accounts are grim.[45] Private William Murphy, who knew the food situation well, had this to say:

> During the winter of 1866 and 1867 the bacon and flour I had seen at Reno was given to us. The flour had been hauled sixty-five miles and handled several times. The result was that the refuse left by the mice was well mixed with the flour and we found a number of dead mice in it also. As we could not get a seive, we manufactured one out of a burlap sack by pulling out some of the strings and nailing it on a wooden frame. We got most of the larger refuse out. The bacon, where the fat had commenced to sluff off from the lean was yellow with age and bitter as quinine. Some of the worst we shaved off, but we could not spare too much.[46]

[40] Margaret Carrington, *Absaraka*, p. 41.
[41] Murphy, "Forgotten Battalion," p. 387.
[42] Margaret Carrington, *Absaraka*, p. 165.
[43] *Ibid.*, pp. 203–204.
[44] Murphy, "Forgotten Battalion," p. 392.
[45] Samuel S. Gibson, "The Wagon Box Fight," in Hebard and Brininstool, *The Bozeman Trail*, p. 39.
[46] Murphy, "Forgotten Battalion," p. 387.

Citizen hunters provided a brief respite from this diet on February 13, 1867, when they sold 1,270 pounds of buffalo meat to the Acting Commissary of Subsistence.[47] But flour supplies dwindled and in early March the ration was further reduced.[48]

Spring opened up the roads to wagon traffic, and antiscorbutics (potatoes, onions, pickled vegetables, and molasses) came up the trail to Fort Philip Kearny on March 17.[49] As the countryside became green, men with scurvy went afield for wild onions. Forbidden to do so by an order from Department headquarters they ". . . went out just the same. We thought we might just as well die at once as to die by inches."[50]

Except for the Charles Washington family at Fort Philip Kearny, there is no evidence that any gardens were planted at either post.

Flour remained in short supply into the summer; special instructions were issued controlling the sale of flour to laundresses; and children were put on a reduced flour ration. Scurvy continued to be a problem in the summer, although it was alleviated to some degree by extra issues of sauerkraut, pickled cabbage, pickles, dried apples, and molasses.[51]

The quantity, quality, and variety of foods improved sharply in the fall of 1867 at both posts. Men in the hayfields and in the Pinery hunted buffalo, antelope, sage hen, and bear, supplementing the increased quantities of rationed items.[52] Stores of antiscorbutics available for issue included dried apples, dried peaches, molasses, syrup, cucumber pickles, mixed pickles, onion pickles, cabbages, onions, curried cabbage, and sauerkraut.[53] Fresh potatoes and onions arrived at the posts in large quantity up to late November and early December, 1867, packed in sawdust to prevent freezing.[54]

---

[47] Special Order Number 32, Headquarters, Fort Philip Kearny, February 13, 1867, NARS, RG 98.

[48] General Order Number 20, Headquarters, Fort Philip Kearny, February 13, 1867, NARS, RG 98.

[49] Record of Events, Post Return for March, 1867, Fort Philip Kearny, NARS, RG 98.

[50] Murphy, "Forgotten Battalion," p. 393.

[51] Special Order Number 123, Headquarters, Fort Philip Kearny, July 24, 1867, NARS, RG 98; General Orders, Number 53 and Number 54, Headquarters, Fort Philip Kearny, August 4, 1867, NARS, RG 98.

[52] Wishart "Diary," August 30, September 9, 11, 12, and October 12, 1867; Frederic Claus, "My Experience in the Wagon Box Fight," in Hebard and Brininstool, *Bozeman Trail*, II, 86.

[53] "A list of anti-scorbutics at the Post Commissary, Fort Philip Kearny, D.T., on hand October 31, 1867," by First Lieutenant C. H. Warrens, Regimental Quartermaster and Acting Commissary of Subsistence, NARS, RG 98, LR, Fort Philip Kearny.

[54] "Summaries of Receipts of Commissary Stores," Fort Philip Kearny, 1867, NARS, RG 98, LR, Fort Philip Kearny; Special Order Number 126, Headquarters, Fort Reno, November 23, 1867, NARS, RG 98.

Supplies of nonrationed items carried by the Acting Commissary of Subsistence increased also, with canned tomatoes, oysters, peaches, jelly, jam, and vinegar all arriving in great quantity. The post commander allowed civilian employees to purchase commissary supplies without paying the transportation cost, and this virtually doubled their purchasing power.[55] Corn meal was in such ample supply that it was fed to the beef cattle that winter.[56]

Beef cattle arrived at Fort Reno in January, 1868, but they were Texas cattle and would not eat corn, so they were killed and hung to freeze in the old quartermaster's storehouse until issued.[57] To supplement the fresh meat supply and clean out surplus stores of other kinds in April, 1868, Van Voast ordered that the "Post Commissary will purchase from 'Sorrel Horse,' Chief of the Arapahoes, the buffalo meat which he has brought to the post, and will sell to said chief such commissary stores as can be spared, charging cost and transportation."[58]

Clearly, then, the miscalculations and poor planning that resulted in so much suffering the first quarter of 1867 were temporary, and the army learned rather quickly to handle the problem of adequate food supplies for the Powder River posts.

WATER

Although a good water supply was never a problem at Fort Philip Kearny, with the Pineys close at hand, Fort Reno was plagued from beginning to end. Bad water is endemic in the country along the main Powder River and along most of the small streams between it and the North Platte River. Connor's men got "good wells at 20 feet," in August, 1865,[59] but these soon failed, and by the following summer of 1866 the volunteers were again dependent on the alkaline and muddy water of the Powder, which they had to haul up the steep hill by wagon. The Carrington command discovered a spring near the

[55] Special Order Number 187, Headquarters, Fort Philip Kearny, November 6, 1867, NARS, RG 98.
[56] Special Order Number 210, Headquarters, Fort Philip Kearny, December 16, 1867, NARS, RG 98.
[57] Special Order Number 5, Headquarters, Fort Reno, January 9, 1868, NARS, RG 98.
[58] Special Order Number 53, Headquarters, Fort Reno, April 17, 1868, NARS, RG 98.
[59] Captain B. F. Rockafellow, 6th Michigan Volunteer Cavalry, "Diary," August 15, 1865, in Hafen and Hafen, *Powder River Campaigns and Sawyer's Expedition*, p. 180.

base of the bluff that lasted at least until the departure of their main
column, on July 10, 1866.[60] Carrington wrote from Fort Reno that
on their march no good water could be obtained, except by digging,
for the last one hundred miles.[61] Gray Eagle, Carrington's favorite
horse, died, its demise attributed to bad water on this stretch of
the march.[62] Van Voast noted in August, 1867, that his inex-
perienced men were unable to reach water, and an experienced
civilian well-digger was hired at carpenter's wages to make the
attempt.[63] Significantly, one of the main reasons for abandoning
the Cantonment Reno-Fort McKinney No. One site, three miles
from Fort Reno, was this water problem (see Chapters 7 and 9 on
this post).

CLOTHING

Uniforms were in generally good supply at both posts. Carrington
issued new uniforms to each man after completion of the heavy
construction work in October, 1866, but the Boards of Survey noted
at the time that they were all issued at reduced charges, since mice
and moths had tunneled through the clothing bales.[64] In the spring
of 1868, the quartermasters at the posts sold clothing to civilian employees at cost plus transportation in order to reduce the stock on
hand prior to abandoning the posts.[65]

The principal problem with clothing was that the standard uniform
did not adapt well to the extremes of High Plains weather.[66] More than
thirty years of experimentation lay ahead before a suitable variety of
well-designed uniform components would be available.[67]

[60] Margaret Carrington, *Absaraka*, p. 107.
[61] Henry B. Carrington to Adjutant General, Department of the Platte, July 1,
1866, NARS, RG 98, LR, Department of the Platte.
[62] James Carrington, "Across the Plains with Bridger as Guide," *Scribners*,
LXXXV, Number 1 (January 1929).
[63] Special Order Number 60, Headquarters, Fort Reno, August 2, 1867, NARS,
RG 98.
[64] Reports of Boards of Survey, 1866, Fort Philip Kearny, NARS, RG 98, LR,
Fort Philip Kearny.
[65] Special Order Number 40, Headquarters, Fort Philip Kearny, April 15, 1868,
NARS, RG 98.
[66] Murphy, "Forgotten Battalion," p. 392.
[67] Gordon S. Chappell, *The Search for the Well-Dressed Soldier, 1865–1890* (Tucson,
Arizona: The Sun Dance Co., 1964); Don Rickey, Jr., *Forty Miles a Day on Beans
and Hay* (Norman: University of Oklahoma Press, 1963), pp. 122–126; Sidney B.
Brinckerhoff, *Military Headgear in the Southwest, 1846–1890* (Tucson, Arizona:
Arizona Pioneers Historical Society, 1965).

FORAGE

Good transport depended on healthy animals, and their health was governed largely by the available forage. Regulations provided for the following daily allowances: horses, fourteen pounds of hay, twelve pounds of oats, corn, or barley; mules, fourteen pounds of hay, nine pounds of oats, corn, or barley.[68] Corn, which could be densely packed and was high in nutritional value, was the preferred grain for shipment to the remote posts.[69] The Chief Quartermaster, Department of the Platte, usually bought the corn in Omaha—then near the western limit of commercial corn culture—and issued contracts for its transportation to the army posts. The cost of transportation alone from Omaha to Fort Philip Kearny was twelve to thirteen cents per pound, for corn in the usual 125-pound sacks.[70]

Two successive transportation contractors defaulted in 1866 and 1867 by refusing to transport corn farther than the country around Fort Laramie. The first was a man named D. I. McCann. The second was better known, "the notorious Colonel Chivington of Sand Creek Massacre Memory," with his subcontractors Lang and Willard.[71] Due to their failure to deliver corn to Fort Philip Kearny, horses of the cavalry and mounted infantry were in poor condition by October.[72]

The volunteers at Fort Reno had little stock and evidently cut no hay before they left in July, 1866. Carrington found that "for 20 miles about this post no hay can be cut, and sagebrush and cacti form the great feature of the vegetation, while the grasshoppers are rapidly destroying what else is available."[73]

Carrington noted, in contrast, the fine meadows along the Piney and neighboring streams. The close herding of hundreds of mules, horses, and oxen after the first Indian attacks quickly depleted nearby resources. The firm of Coe and Carter were hay contractors for the post, delivering hay at $100 to $128 per ton. Their hay parties required

[68] 1121, Revised Army Regulations, Adjutant General's Office (Washington, D.C.: 1861 edition).

[69] Quartermaster's records of the posts and Boards of Survey on the receipt of stores indicate that no other kind of grain was ever received there.

[70] Colonel I. N. Palmer to Adjutant General, Department of the Platte, March 16, 1867, NARS, RG 98, LR, Department of the Platte; Boards of Survey, Quartermaster stores, Fort Reno and Fort Philip Kearny, 1866–1868, NARS, RG 98.

[71] *Ibid.*

[72] Henry B. Carrington to Adjutant General, Department of the Platte, September 17 and 25, 1866, NARS, RG 98, LR, Department of the Platte.

[73] *Ibid.*, June 28, 1866.

a guard of forty men at five dollars per day, plus high pay and costly rations for the hay cutters themselves. At the time, officers and civilians alike thought the price was justified.[74] Untimely rains, prairie fires, and Indian depredations all hampered haying operations in the fall of 1866. By the end of November, Carrington reduced hay issues from fourteen pounds to eight pounds per animal per day.[75]

Mules at Fort Philip Kearny were near starvation in January, and were gnawing the logs of their stables. The men stopped this by covering the posts with green hides, turned flesh side out.[76] Borrowing from Indian practice, they cut large quantities of green cottonwood along the Piney, and fed the tops to the stock.[77] With considerable hardship a small party went to Fort Reno for some corn early in February, but at the cost of reducing that post's corn ration to four pounds per day per animal.[78] Several weeks later an emergency shipment of twenty-five wagonfuls of corn (about fifty thousand pounds, light loaded for winter travel) went up the trail from Fort Laramie.[79] Fairly simple calculation reveals that it must have taken over half that quantity to get the mules of the train to Fort Philip Kearny and back to Fort Laramie.

Wessells made an attempt in late February to save as many horses as possible by transferring Company C, 2nd Cavalry, to Fort Laramie. They took with them all unserviceable horses and mules.[80] On March 17, Company L, 2nd Cavalry, was ordered transferred to Fort Laramie, taking with them all but twenty of the best horses at Fort Philip Kearny.[81] Many of these died on the road, and Colonel Palmer at Fort Laramie charged that the contractors' default had brought about

[74] Special Order Number 69, Headquarters, Fort Philip Kearny, November 17, 1866, NARS, RG 98; John Bratt, *Trails of Yesterday*, p. 87.

[75] Henry B. Carrington to Adjutant General, Department of the Platte, September 17 and 25, 1866, NARS, RG 98, LR, Department of the Platte; Special Order Number 45, Headquarters, Fort Philip Kearny, October 11, 1866, NARS, RG 98; Special Order Number 69, Headquarters, Fort Philip Kearny, November 17, 1866, NARS, RG 98; Special Order Number 81, Headquarters, Fort Philip Kearny, November 30, 1866, NARS, RG 98.

[76] Fessenden, "Personal Experiences in and around Fort Phil Kearny," p. 105.

[77] Murphy, "Forgotten Battalion," pp. 391–392.

[78] Special Order Number 25, Headquarters, Fort Philip Kearny, February 2, 1867, NARS, RG 98; Special Order Number 12, Headquarters, Fort Reno, February 5, 1867, NARS, RG 98.

[79] Colonel I. N. Palmer, at Fort Laramie, to Brevet Brigadier General Wessells, Fort Philip Kearny, February 5, 1867, NARS, RG 98, LS, Fort Laramie.

[80] Special Order Number 35, Headquarters, Fort Philip Kearny, February 17 1867, NARS, RG 98.

[81] Special Order Number 49, Headquarters, Fort Philip Kearny, March 17, 1867, NARS, RG 98.

the death of thirty thousand dollars worth of government stock at Fort Philip Kearny and Fort Reno.[82]

ARMS AND AMMUNITION

Connor's column came into the Powder River country well armed and well supplied with ammunition. The 6th Michigan Volunteer Cavalry companies intended as a garrison for Fort Connor had the .56 caliber Spencer carbine of Civil War fame. The infantry, including Companies C and D, 5th U.S. Volunteers, were armed with the standard .58 caliber Springfield rifle musket, the basic infantry arm of the Civil War.[83]

Carrington's 18th Infantry carried the same .58 caliber Springfield rifle musket. Company C, 2nd Cavalry, arriving at Fort Philip Kearny in October, 1866, had Starr carbines and a few Springfields. The 18th Infantry Regimental Band obtained Spencer carbines, presumably the .56 caliber Civil War type, at Fort Kearny, Nebraska, in the spring of 1866. Carrington used these carbines to replace the Springfields and Starrs of Company C, 2nd Cavalry.[84]

Cavalry units arriving in 1867–1868 should have had the Model 1865 .50 caliber Spencer carbine, standard at this time.

Colonel John E. Smith, 27th Infantry, arrived at Fort Reno on June 29 and at Fort Philip Kearny on July 3, 1867, with his trains carrying the new Model 1866 Springfield breech-loading rifle musket. The last of the .58 caliber Springfields in the hands of troops were exchanged for the new breechloaders on August 12, when Company E, 27th Infantry, arrived at Fort Philip Kearny from escort duty.[85]

[82] Colonel I. N. Palmer, at Fort Laramie, to Inspector General, Department of the Platte, May 18, 1867, NARS, RG 98, LR, Department of the Platte.

[83] Rockafellow, "Diary," p. 169; William B. Edwards, *Civil War Guns* (Harrisburg, Pennsylvania: Stackpole, 1962); Claud E. Fuller, *The Rifle Musket* (Harrisburg, Pennsylvania: Stackpole, 1958). Both books give the best data on this weapon.

[84] Henry B. Carrington to Adjutant General, Department of the Platte, June 16, 1866, NARS, RG 98, LR, Department of the Platte; Major James Van Voast, at Fort Laramie, to Adjutant General, Department of the Platte, September 26 and October 20, 1866, NARS, RG 98, LR, Department of the Platte; Murphy, "Forgotten Battalion," p. 389; Henry B. Carrington to Adjutant General, Department of the Platte, April 26, 1866, NARS, RG 98, LR, Department of the Platte; Henry B. Carrington, statement in Senate Executive Document 33, 50th Cong., 1st Sess., p. 45.

[85] Brevet Major John R. Edie, Chief Ordnance Officer, Department of the Platte, to Colonel John E. Smith, at Fort Laramie, en route to Fort Philip Kearny, May 21, 1867, NARS, RG 98, LS, Department of the Platte; Special Order Number 134, Headquarters, Fort Philip Kearny, August 12, 1867, NARS, RG 98.

Revolvers were considered the standard side arm for cavalry at this time. The well proved .44 caliber Colt and Remington Civil War models were both used at these posts.

Officers occasionally carried nonstandard arms. Carrington had a "near standard" .36 caliber "Navy" Colt, very popular with officers at the time.[86] Lieutenant Alexander Wishart had a .32 caliber Smith and Wesson rim-fire pocket revolver. Lieutenant Link used a Henry, and Chaplain David White is supposed to have charged the Indians once at Crazy Woman Fork armed with a "pepperbox."[87]

Some comment on these arms and their tactical implications seems in order. The 1863 .58 caliber rifle musket was the final development of a series of new arms of that caliber adopted in 1855. Its Minié hollow-base elongated bullet, small enough to ram down the bore easily, expanded on firing to engage the rifling. These rifles could be fired about three aimed shots per minute by trained troops. They had much greater long-range accuracy and a flatter trajectory than previous round-ball arms. Such arms were first used against Indians on the Blue Water by Harney's men in 1855. The production of the rifle musket and its ammunition was well standardized by 1865. Though outclassed by some late Civil War contract arms, it remained an effective infantry weapon, better by far than the miscellany of smoothbore trade muskets that formed the main armament of the Indian at this time. As will be seen, it was much more lack of training than poor arms that caused the soldier of 1866 to be at a disadvantage and to lack self-confidence.[88]

Replacing the .58 caliber rifle musket in July, 1866, the .50–70 caliber Springfield breech-loading rifle musket was a fine weapon. It was simple and sturdy, using the same lock, stock, and small hardware as its predecessor. The breech-loading "trap door" mechanism speeded loading and made possible about double the rate of accurate fire. More important was the ease of loading in a sitting or prone position behind cover. The sturdy waterproof metal cartridge cut down loss and damage of ammunition in the field. Flatter trajectory

[86] Frances Carrington, in *My Army Life*, describes the incident in which the Colonel's revolver accidentally discharged due to a broken safety-stop pin between the chambers, and identifies the revolver as this type.

[87] Wishart, "Diary," memorandum inventory of a box shipped from home, listing cartridges for this model revolver; Fessenden, "Personal Experiences in and around Fort Phil Kearny, p. 91; Frances Carrington, *My Army Life*.

[88] Edwards, *Civil War Guns*, presents a fine discussion of the performance and tactical implications of the rifle musket.

made long-range hits easier. Convenience of loading simplified training, allowing more time for actual target practice.

The Starr single-shot breech-loading carbine carried by the men of Company C, 2nd Cavalry, on their arrival was a simple, reliable weapon, using the same ammunition as the Spencer. The fights in December, 1866, may have been the last combat use of the Starr by the regular army, as the miscellany of Civil War carbines were now being phased out in favor of the standard Spencer.

Spencer carbines had widespread use in the Civil War and were among the best of the Civil War carbines. The Civil War version is called the .56 caliber, but this is actually the diameter of the cartridge case, the bullet being around .54 caliber. The 1865 model Spencer had an improved cartridge with a longer case to cover the lubricating grooves so that cartridge would stay cleaner. Actual caliber, charge, and performance level were much the same as the earlier model, and easy manufacturing tolerances made the ammunition of both models interchangeable.[89] At Fort Reno and Fort Philip Kearny the Spencer was both serviceable and trouble free. An abundance of Spencer ammunition, left at Fort Reno by the Connor column, enhanced the Spencers' usefulness. Elsewhere in the army, some contract lots of ammunition gave trouble in these guns. Other factors, such as the demise of the company that manufactured it and the desire of the army for a more powerful carbine led to the obsolescence of the Spencer in 1869.

The Colt and Remington army revolvers were fine weapons, though of limited usefulness in most western combat situations. They were most useful to working parties who could not always keep a rifle or carbine handy. Unfortunately they were in shortest supply at the Powder River posts at just the period in 1866 when they were most needed.[90]

The Fort Reno garrison had at hand in 1865–1866 six pieces of artillery, specifically one twelve-pounder field howitzer and five twelve-pounder mountain howitzers with ammunition.[91] Carrington took the field howitzer and three of the mountain howitzers to Fort Philip Kearny with some ammunition. Early in October, he received

[89] *Ibid.*; A. F. Lustyik, *Civil War Carbines* (Aledo, Illinois: The Gun Report, Inc., 1962).

[90] In this early period, July–September, 1866, there is no indication that anyone but officers had revolvers, and only the cavalry appear to have had them after this time.

[91] Brown, *Galvanized Yankees*, pp. 133–134.

a large amount of additional ammunition making the guns relatively well supplied.[92] The howitzers had a reasonable amount of use, generally with the "spherical case" projectile. The mountain howitzer could use these with good effect to eight hundred yards and the field howitzer had a range of well over a thousand yards. A time fuse fired the bursting charge with precision, scattering iron fragments and lead filler-balls at high velocity. The Indians soon learned to respect these little guns. So much so, that by 1867, Colonel John E. Smith wished for a Three-Inch Ordnance Rifle with which to surprise them at extreme range.[93]

Carrington complained frequently of a shortage of .58 caliber rifle-musket ammunition. On arrival at Fort Reno he had a stock of sixty thousand rounds.[94] He left some of this with the force there, and sent some on to Fort C. F. Smith, but on or before September 17, 1866, he received sixty thousand more rounds, and in early October, thirty-eight thousand more, giving him a normal supply.[95] Even after the Fetterman fight, there may have been two hundred rounds to the gun for the Springfields, and abundant ammunition for such Starr and Spencer carbines as remained.[96]

Clearly, the troops at Fort Philip Kearny and Fort Reno were as well supplied as any troops in the West at this period, and certainly much better supplied than their Indian enemy. It is equally clear, however, that in 1865 and 1866 few of the men were trained well enough to use these arms effectively.

FUEL

Both Fort Reno and Fort Philip Kearny were fortunate in having cooking and heating fuel reasonably close at hand. Many frontier

[92] Record of Events, Post Return for August, 1866, Fort Philip Kearny, NARS, RG 98; telegram, Van Voast, at Fort Laramie, to Adjutant General, Department of the Platte, September 27, 1866, NARS, RG 98, LR, Department of the Platte.

[93] Margaret Carrington, *Absaraka*, p. 149; Colonel John E. Smith to Adjutant General, Department of the Platte, July 28, 1867, NARS, RG 98, LR, Department of the Platte.

[94] Henry B. Carrington to Adjutant General, Department of the Platte, June 16, 1866, NARS, RG 98, LR, Department of the Platte.

[95] Henry B. Carrington to Adjutant General, Department of the Platte, September 17, 1866, NARS, RG 98, LR, Department of the Platte; telegram, Major James Van Voast, at Fort Laramie, to Adjutant General, Department of the Platte, September 27, 1866, NARS, RG 98, LR, Department of the Platte.

[96] James Van Voast, at Fort Laramie, to Henry B. Carrington, August 11, 1866, NARS, RG 98, LS, Fort Laramie; Henry B. Carrington to Adjutant General, Department of the Platte, July 30, 1866, NARS, RG 98, LS, Fort Laramie.

posts of this era were plagued with serious fuel shortages. Fort Sedgwick, Colorado, paid from $75 to $105 per cord of wood in this period.[97] By contrast, Fort Reno had abundant standing and fallen cottonwood just across the river, and wood could usually be secured by troop labor.[98] Because of some problem with contractors at Fort Philip Kearny the army did not secure enough firewood in the fall of 1866, and details of enlisted men cut green cottonwood along the Piney for their own fires, and frequently went to the Pinery to cut pine wood to build the officers' quarters.[99] The quartermaster purchased small quantities of wood that winter at $20.00 per cord.[100]

Two civilian miners, hired at $35.00 per month, got out some lignite below the post along the Little Piney from March to June, 1867.[101]

The fuel situation, as with other supplies, improved in 1867. Early in November there were 3,400 cords of wood on hand, bought at $27.50 per cord, from contractor Fred Weddle.[102] N. M. Meredith delivered 480 tons of lignite at $16.66 per ton, and another 500 tons were bought on open-market purchase at $6.00 per ton.[103] Eight hundred bushels of charcoal for blacksmith's work cost $2.00 per bushel.[104] Some of the contractors mentioned above delivered supplies in smaller quantity to Fort Reno on their way down the trail to winter their stock.[105]

[97] James F. Rusling, "Report of Inspection of Fort Sedgwick, Colorado Territory," House Executive Document 45, 39th Cong., 2nd Sess., p. 31.

[98] Report of William B. Hazen to Adjutant General, Department of the Platte, sent from Fort Reno, August 22, 1866, NARS, RG 98, LR, Department of the Platte; Major E. B. Grimes to Chief Quartermaster, Department of the Platte, "Inspection Report of Fort Reno," November 11 and 12, 1867 (sent from Fort Laramie, December 2, 1867), NARS, RG 98, LR, Department of the Platte.

[99] Murphy, "Forgotten Battalion," pp. 391–392; Gibson, "The Wagon Box Fight," pp. 39–71.

[100] Special Order Number 97, Headquarters, Fort Philip Kearny, December 31, 1866, NARS, RG 98.

[101] Record of Events, Post Returns, March through June, 1867, NARS, RG 98, Fort Philip Kearny; entry in Communications Register, January 15, 1867, relative to coal sources, NARS, RG 98.

[102] Board of Survey, receipt of wood from Gilmore and Porter, Fort Philip Kearny, November 13, 1867, NARS, RG 98, LR, Fort Philip Kearny; Special Order Number 106, Headquarters, Fort Reno, October 17, 1867, NARS, RG 98; Special Order Number 110, Headquarters, Fort Reno, October 24, 1867, NARS, RG 98.

[103] Special Order Number 194, Headquarters, Fort Philip Kearny, November 19, 1867, NARS, RG 98; Grimes, "Inspection Report of Fort Reno"; Special Order Number 201, Headquarters, Fort Philip Kearny, November 29, 1867, NARS, RG 98.

[104] Reports of Boards of Survey, NARS, RG 98, LR, Fort Philip Kearny, 1867.

[105] Reports of Boards of Survey, NARS, RG 98, LR, Fort Reno, 1867.

Fort Reno and Fort Philip Kearny, then, were well staffed throughout their occupancy. During 1867 and 1868, training continually
improved the effectiveness of the forces garrisoned there, and the
material resources available improved in both quantity and quality
with the improvement of transportation throughout the period.

Chapter 5. Operations in the Powder River Country from the Close of the Connor Campaign to the Abandonment of the Early Posts

The nature of operations at the early Powder River posts can be divided into four periods, each characterized by the composition of the garrison and the personality of the key officers.

OPERATIONS OF THE VOLUNTEERS, AUGUST, 1865–JUNE, 1866

In Fort Connor's first week as a post General Connor camped across the river, while a certain amount of active patroling went on:

> There is a trail six miles west of here over which they [the Indians] pass, and not being aware of our presence, we sometimes get one. Yesterday my scouts killed one of the principal chiefs of the Cheyennes, and today Captain Marshall, Eleventh Ohio, killed two Indians.[1]

Connor's departure brought an end to this air of energy, optimism, and activity. Construction work continued, since this was a matter of personal survival as well as comfort. As the "collection of cottonwood shacks" reached completion, the garrison settled down to a simple winter routine. Having no direction and no policy except to hold the fort, the men had little incentive. The men of Companies C and D, 5th U.S. Volunteers, merely wanted to drift through the long winter until their mustering out. The Winnebagos had at least a quiet, comfortable existence. Both faced an uncertain future.[2]

---

[1] Connor to Dodge, August 21, 1865, in Leroy R. Hafen and Ann W. Hafen, editors, *The Powder River Campaigns and Sawyer's Expedition, 1865* (Glendale, California: The Arthur H. Clark Co., 1961).

[2] John Ryan of Buffalo, Wyoming, quoted by T. J. Gatchell in "Events of the Year 1865 Pertaining to Johnson County," *Annals of Wyoming*, XXVII, Number 2 (October 1955), 141.

There were no regular officers at the post, thus even the traditional leadership and stimuli of garrison life were missing. The volunteer officers simplified post routing as much as possible, and formal calls were limited to:

> Reveille: daylight.
> Breakfast: 7:30 A.M.
> Surgeon's call: 8:00 A.M.
> Dinner call: 12:00 noon.
> Retreat: sunset.
> Guard mount: immediately following retreat.
> Tattoo: 8:00 P.M.[3]

There was no training, no drill, and little relief from the daily boredom. Cutting wood, hauling water, feeding the stock, issuing rations, caring for the sick, and waiting, waiting, waiting, was about all the men could do.

They may have been paid but once before their relief in the summer of 1866. No women, no liquor, only a little gambling, and even that was intermittently suppressed.

OPERATIONS—CARRINGTON, JUNE, 1866–JANUARY, 1867

The Carrington column entered the Powder River country charged with the task of building posts along the Bozeman Trail, keeping their lines of supply and communication open, and increasing the safety of the trail to travelers. They were enjoined not to start a full-scale Indian war and to teach the Indians respect for the army while at the same time not to tolerate Indian aggression. These were complex and contradictory goals, but such are the tactics of limited warfare.

Colonel Henry B. Carrington, 18th Infantry, commanded the Mountain District through the third quarter of 1866, and continued to command all the troops in the District for the balance of that year. He brought to the work a curious assortment of resources and handicaps. An energetic man, forty-two years old, a Yale graduate and successful lawyer, Carrington had five years' service, all as colonel, in the 18th Infantry. His outright appointment to this position was clearly a reward for hard political work in the formative years of Ohio's Republican party.[4] However, his appointment to the regulars

---

[3] Special Order Number 3, Headquarters, Fort Connor, October 28, 1865, NARS, RG 98.

[4] M. M. Quaife, "Historical Introduction," in Margaret I. Carrington, *Absaraka, Home of the Crows* (Chicago: Lakeside Press, 1950), pp. xxvi–xxviii.

only undermined his relationship with the true professionals of the regular army.

Carrington's ambition, intellect, and energy enabled him to absorb a vast amount of detailed military literature. When he arrived in the Powder River country, he possessed a wealth of textbook knowledge of regulations, military engineering, artillery, and administrative paper work. He had, unfortunately, never had the opportunity to practice any of this under field conditions!—and the situation at hand required that he do so immediately. He proved that he could apply his technical knowledge to many practical problems speedily and effectively. The completed fort on the Piney stood as testimony to this, as did his demonstration of skill as an artilleryman.

Beyond this, however, his shortcomings appear more frequently. Always more contemplative than decisive, he could not thread his way through the tangle of army red tape and adjust his operations effectively to it. Ever the hopeful humanitarian, he proved extremely naive when dealing with Indians, officers, and soldiers. He seems to have assigned officers to duties that he hoped would improve them, rather than to duties that would put their skills to productive use. When they failed, he all too often took on their tasks himself. Generally poor at delegating authority, he was soon not only district commander and colonel of the 18th Infantry, but post commander, engineer, draftsman, construction supervisor, and for all practical purposes, battalion commander, moral arbiter, and guidance specialist. Yet he still felt compelled to make the rounds of guard posts nightly![5] A personality such as this inevitably affected the entire command and had an impact on all phases of operations.

The command that Carrington led into the Powder River country contained both raw recruits and seasoned veterans. Both faced a new kind of enemy and a new kind of warfare. From an army conditioned to massive supply, they stood at the lonely end of a tenuous and expensive supply line, facing an enemy to whom "wilderness survival" was the routine course of existence. The soldier was conditioned to think in terms of taking and holding ground, while to the Indian holding ground militarily meant nothing. Civil War experience conditioned the soldier to expect to "fight a war" or "maintain a peace," but the Indian's whole way of life was built around a state of continuous warfare, and he viewed the white soldier as he viewed his

[5] Henry B. Carrington to Adjutant General, Department of the Platte, July 30, 1866, NARS, RG 98, LR, Department of the Platte.

neighboring enemy tribes, as a resource to be exploited continuously, rather than as a foe to be driven from the land forever.

Nevertheless, the army possessed numerous basic advantages. Most important was a strategic view of the Indian question. At the tactical level, there was the framework for organization, discipline, and planning. And the army possessed a vast superiority in weapons and ammunition and the means to constantly replenish this supply.

The best offensive advantage of the Indian was his ability to use cover and concealment as a surprise tactic. His greatest weakness was his lack of even a rudimentary standing tactical organization. His mobility and his abundance of tough and expendable horses constituted his prime defense.

The Sioux treated both the emigrant and the soldier to the same sort of warfare they carried on against the Crows, the Assiniboines, and the Shoshonis. Their main target was the horse herd. Four generations of practice made these red men the most proficient horse thieves in Plains history. The large, well-proportioned American horses were tempting targets, and if a careless citizen or soldier strayed in their path, so much the better—for guns, ammunition, coups, and scalps were welcome, too! The horse raid and its assorted outgrowths formed the typical engagement of this early period. Attempts to overrun small parties and decoy forces into ambush developed only after the troops persistently displayed their vulnerability.

The citizen parties Carrington found traveling along the Bozeman Trail in the summer of 1866 were often ill prepared for the frontier. Diverse in background, united only in a desire to get to the gold mines, they were poorly equipped, contentious, and disorganized—a far cry indeed from the frontier people of a generation earlier. Carrington and the other post commanders commented on this, and generally attempted to instill a certain amount of caution and organization into these parties.[6] Carrington issued orders governing the emigrant trains:

> Thirty armed men constitute a party, which upon selection of its commander or conductor, will be allowed to proceed. The reduction of this number will depend upon the general conduct of trains and the condition and safety of the route, of which due notice will be given.
>
> When a train shall have organized, the conductor will present to the post

[6] Henry B. Carrington, comments in Sen. Exec. Doc. 33, 50th Cong., 1st Sess., p. 7.

commander a list of the men accompanying the said train, upon which list, if satisfactory, he will endorse "Permission given to pass to Fort Reno." Upon arrival of a train at Fort Reno, the conductor will report with his list, indorsed as above mentioned, to the post commander to receive the same indorsed approval as in the first instance to pass to the next post. This examination and approval must be had at each post, so that the last post commander on the Upper Yellowstone will have the evidence that the train has passed all posts.

The constant separation and scattering of trains pretending to act in concert must be stopped; and for the information of emigrants and well-disposed citizens the following reasons are given, viz: First, nearly all danger from Indians lies in the recklessness of travelers. A small party, when separated, either sell whiskey to or fire upon scattering Indians, or get in dispute with them and somebody is hurt. An insult to an Indian is resented by the Indians against the first white men they meet, and innocent travelers suffer.

Again, the new route is short and will be made perfectly secure. The co-operation of citizens is therefore essential for their own personal comfort as well as for the interests of the public at large; and if citizens ask, as they will of course rightly expect, the protection and aid from Government troops, they must themselves be equally diligent in avoiding difficulties with the Indians, or among themselves. . . .[7]

However, such orders were hard to enforce, and citizens continued to wander away from their wagons and pose as unwitting targets to the roaming war parties. Most of the citizen and soldier casualties throughout the early period occurred in this way.[8]

At Fort Reno, Carrington had his first experience with what was to become a common occurrence. Indians would run off the sutler's horse and mule herd, and seventy of Carrington's mounted detachment would pelt off in pursuit, only to return hours later with one abandoned Indian pony and a mere handful of trade goods to show for their ride.[9]

Neither Carrington nor his successors were ever given the manpower, the logistic support, or the authority to carry on effective offensive operations. Thus clearly committed to the defensive, they

[7] General Order Number 4, Headquarters, Mountain District, June 30, 1866, NARS, RG 98.

[8] Telegram, Henry B. Carrington to Adjutant General, Department of the Platte, July 30, 1866, NARS, RG 98, LR, Department of the Platte; Henry B. Carrington to Adjutant General, Department of the Platte, July 30, 1866, NARS, RG 98, LR, Department of the Platte; telegram, Henry B. Carrington to Adjutant General, Department of the Platte, August 29, 1866, NARS, RG 98, LR, Department af the Platte.

[9] Henry B. Carrington, comments in Sen. Exec. Doc. 33, 50th Cong., 1st Sess., pp. 6–7.

had to evolve tactics which would secure their property and at the same time give them the freedom of movement to carry out their other tasks. Unfortunately, it was in just this basic task that Carrington and his command failed.

The Carrington command fortified an already advantageous position at Fort Reno. They constructed the substantial Fort Philip Kearny, and the plain-looking, but effective Fort C. F. Smith. Three blockhouses were built at the Pinery west of Fort Philip Kearny. The widely approved blockhouses at points along the line of communications (at Cheyenne River, Crazy Woman, and Tongue River), and a post at the crossing of the Upper Yellowstone were not built, mainly because Carrington did not feel he had sufficient manpower.[10] Hazen, on the other hand, experienced in Indian fighting himself, thought that two companies were a sufficient garrison for each post and its outposts, and that thirty men could hold any post along the line if some men were withdrawn for active field operations.[11]

Carrington did build reasonably well, all things considered. Too well, if anything, in view of the well-known reluctance of the Plains Indians to attack fortified positions. Perhaps *some* of the thousands of man-hours involved in building Fort Philip Kearny's defenses might have been diverted to training, which could form the basis for a truly effective defense. Drill was not regularly scheduled at Fort Philip Kearny at any time in the Carrington period. Twice, battalion-massed formations were practiced.[12] Lest the reader object that drill was of little value on the frontier, he should remember that most of the men carried the 1863 Springfield rifle musket. Loading this weapon effectively and rapidly in combat required instinctive mastery of a sequence called the loadings and firings. This mastery could only be gained by precise and repetitive drill.[13] There was no target practice at Fort Philip Kearny in Carrington's time.[14] He apparently felt too short of

[10] Henry B. Carrington to Adjutant General, Department of the Platte, August 29; 1866, NARS, RG 98, LR, Department of the Platte; William B. Hazen, in House Executive Document 45, 39th Congress, 1st Session, p. 3; Van Voast, commanding Fort Laramie, to Adjutant General, Department of the Platte, September 10, 1866, NARS, RG 98, LR, Department of the Platte.

[11] Hazen, House Executive Document 45, 39th Cong., 1st Sess., p. 3.

[12] General Order Number 29, Headquarters, Fort Philip Kearny, October 29, 1866, NARS, RG 98; General Order Number 34, November 2, 1866, Fort Philip Kearny, NARS, RG 98.

[13] William B. Edwards, *Civil War Guns* (Harrisburg, Pennsylvania: Stackpole, 1962).

[14] Revised Army Regulations, Adjutant General's Office (Washington, D.C.: 1861 edition), p. 61; William Murphy, "The Forgotten Battalion," *Annals of Wyoming*, VII (October 1930), 391.

ammunition, but after the beginning of October, the supply statistics do not seem to bear him out.[15]

Neither Fort Philip Kearny nor Fort Reno were ever directly attacked at any time. The substantial number of citizen employees and other residents and transients living in cabins and camps on the river bottom were seldom molested. Bailey's mining party was attacked once in daylight, and the Indians were driven off.[16] A party of Indians fired into the contractor's camp on the night of November 3, 1866, but as so often in daylight, they were scared off by howitzer shells.[17]

Wagon trains with few or poorly armed parties were occasionally attacked. As on other frontiers around the world, the corralled wagon train provided a good defense unit. Carrington's wood trains corralled with some frequency, but were never seriously endangered. Better marksmen and the addition of a howitzer with a trained crew might have enabled the wood trains to move with impunity.[18]

By far, the most common type of attack consisted of the sudden dash from under cover at grazing stock—the classic horse raid the Indians specialized in. When the herds were within range of the fort, artillery fire drove them off. However, grass was usually so scarce that the herds had to graze outside this charmed circle. Carrington and his command never developed an effective defense against these surprise attacks. The men were seldom alert to signs of Indians, and often fatally slow to react. Herders were the most frequent casualty. An attack on the herds nearly always brought a force out of the fort, like bees from a hive. Usually, First Lieutenant F. H. Brown, Acting Quartermaster (responsible for the herds and wood trains), and a handful of enlisted men and citizens would charge out the gate of the quartermaster's corral and follow the fleeing Indians for miles without result. On one occasion—September 23, 1866—Brown caught up with a sizable Indian force and a sharp fight ensued. He got back the stock on this occasion by inflicting enough casualties to make the

[15] See Chapter 4 and accompanying notes.

[16] Henry B. Carrington, comments in Sen. Exec. Doc. 33, 50th Cong., 1st Sess., p. 22; Henry B. Carrington to Adjutant General, Department of the Platte, September 25, 1866, NARS, RG 98, LR, Department of the Platte; F. G. Burnett, "Fort C. F. Smith and the Hayfield Fight," in Grace Raymond Hebard and E. A. Brininstool, *The Bozeman Trail* (Glendale, California: The Arthur H. Clark Co., 1960), Vol. II.

[17] Henry B. Carrington to Adjutant General, Department of the Platte, November 5, 1866, NARS, RG 98, LR, Department of the Platte.

[18] Telegram, Henry B. Carrington to Adjutant General, Department of the Platte, October 13, 1866, NARS, RG 98, LR, Department of the Platte.

Indians withdraw, but usually they got away free, sometimes abandoning stock that could not keep up.[19] Occasionally the pursuit was well organized, and an attempt was made to intercept the Indians along their line of retreat. Carrington tried this tactic without result with only fifteen men on September 10, 1866,[20] giving chase for fifteen miles. Ten Eyck, Brown, and Bisbee went out in pursuit a similar distance on the thirteenth.[21] The fights of December 6 and December 21 originated in pursuits that were evidence of ineffective defense tactics.[22]

With the stock in only fair condition in July and August, the troops seldom caught the Indians. As the condition of their mounts declined they did so even less frequently, except when the Indians deliberately sought a fight. Carrington and his officers persisted in responding to minor attacks with these wild pursuits, instead of improving tactical defenses for herds and for small parties in the field. The men individually improved in alertness, but training and discipline were both at such a low level that only the Indians' preoccupation with the herds averted early and heavy casualties in these quick strikes. Generally, the Indians got off with the best stock, and thus the quality of mounts available steadily declined.[23]

The arrival of Company C, 2nd Cavalry, did not improve matters. There is little evidence that they were any more effective than Carrington's mounted infantry detachment, which Hazen had criticized strongly. A few months earlier this same cavalry unit had drawn the following comment:

> The cavalry we now have is bad enough. It requires an officer of experience to be constantly on the watch to preserve his horses and continually repeating instructions in order to beat common sense into some of their heads.
>
> It is the worst cavalry I have ever seen and yet I do not know that any one is to blame. Many are recruits, without instructions—without arms and equipments—with their company commanders constantly changed. . . .[24]

[19] Henry B. Carrington, comments in Sen. Exec. Doc. 33, 50th Cong., 1st Sess., pp. 22–25.

[20] Henry B. Carrington to Adjutant General, Department of the Platte, September 17, 1866, NARS, RG 98, LR, Department of the Platte.

[21] *Ibid.*

[22] See discussion and reports of those fights, cited below.

[23] Henry B. Carrington, comments in Sen. Exec. Doc. 33, 50th Cong., 1st Sess., pp. 22–25.

[24] Van Voast, commanding Fort Laramie, to Adjutant General, Department of the Platte, October 6, 1866, NARS, RG 98, LR, Department of the Platte.

Poor discipline and low morale unquestionably further hampered development of an effective set of defense tactics. Most of the command were on work details fairly continuously during July, August, September, and October. Sometimes they stood guard at night and then worked a full shift during the day.[25] They resented the fact that they were not given the extra duty pay (twenty-five cents to forty cents per day) to which they were entitled, and they felt uneasy over their lack of training, particularly the lack of target practice.[26]

Generally, the men of the command at Fort Philip Kearny and at Fort Reno behaved well, but numerous incidents of insubordination and even of desertion went unpunished. Offenders were frequently arrested for a time, but were usually released without trial, or without the filing of charges.[27] Carrington may have felt compelled to play the role of a reformer. Patient, paternal, and optimistic with the men, he exasperated his officers and NCO's to the limit. He would issue a steady stream of restrictive orders and then fail to provide the necessary support for their enforcement.[28] As a result, company officers increasingly took matters into their own hands, resorting to illegal, sometimes severe, punishment, as the following incident shows.

Lieutenant Bisbee's Company E, 2nd Battalion, 18th Infantry, formed for guard mount on the morning of November 11, 1866. Private John Burke came straggling out of the barracks, delaying the company's departure for the formation. Bisbee then ordered Sergeant Garrett to discipline Burke. Garrett called Burke out of ranks to

---

[25] Henry B. Carrington, from a speech given at the end-of-October ceremonies at Fort Philip Kearny, in Margaret Carrington, *Absaraka*, p. 178.

[26] Murphy, "Forgotten Battalion," pp. 391–395.

[27] Special Order Number 30, Headquarters, Fort Philip Kearny, September 18, 1866, NARS, RG 98; Special Order Number 45, Headquarters, Fort Philip Kearny, October 11, 1866, NARS, RG 98; testimony of Bisbee and Wands, "Proceedings of a Court of Inquiry re: the Fetterman Massacre," 1867, Special File GCMO-002236, Judge Advocate General's Records, NARS, RG 153; Powell's report on Burke's case in third endorsement to Burke's petition for redress of grievance, March 8, 1867, Communication Register and Endorsements, Fort Philip Kearny, NARS, RG 98.

[28] General Order Number 23, Headquarters, Fort Philip Kearny, October 7, 1866, NARS, RG 98; General Order Number 26, Headquarters, Fort Philip Kearny, October 20, 1866, NARS, RG 98; General Order Number 28, Headquarters, Fort Philip Kearny, October 23, 1866, NARS, RG 98; General Order Number 33, Headquarters, Fort Philip Kearny, November 2, 1866, NARS, RG 98; Special Order Number 57, Headquarters, Fort Philip Kearny, November 2, 1866, NARS, RG 98; General Order Number 35, Headquarters, Fort Philip Kearny, November 7, 1866, NARS, RG 98; General Order Number 36, Headquarters, Fort Philip Kearny, November 10, 1866, NARS, RG 98; see Bisbee, Wands, and Powell, cited above, note 27.

reprimand him; Burke snapped out an insolent reply. Garrett thereupon struck Burke with a musket butt, inflicting a skull fracture. Carrington saw the incident and had Garrett arrested and confined, and personally reprimanded Bisbee.[29] Later the same day, he had the widely quoted General Order Number 38 issued and posted, calling the attention of officers and NCO's to the regulations and to humane practice in maintaining discipline.

There was general agreement that although Garrett had gone too far, Carrington's order came months too late, and only in response to intolerable conditions. There is no indication that his disciplinary support for officers and NCO's improved.[30] On December 8, he released Garrett from arrest without filing charges, and during that month he released other men on his own order.[31]

Through the same period of construction at Fort Reno, affairs went more quietly. Ten head of government stock were driven off in three raids, but several attacks on the herds were repulsed without loss.[32] There were a number of reasons for this. Pasture ground and timber were both directly in view of the fort; herds were smaller in relation to the guard force, and repeated successes at Fort Philip Kearny led the Indians to concentrate attacks there, where the pickings had proven richer! The small raiding parties which attacked Fort Reno were seldom pursued because there were not enough mounted men; consequently, there were few skirmishes at a distance.[33]

Indian activity around Fort Philip Kearny subsided somewhat as the Indians concentrated on getting their winter meat. Then, early in December, with their families settled at wintering sites, and the good weather holding out, numerous Indian war parties again took to the field.[34]

The Sioux attacked a wood train on December 6 in what may have been a decoy-ambush plan that broke down, as such plans usually did,

[29] Powell's report, March 8, 1867, cited above, note 27; Special Order Number 64, Headquarters, Fort Philip Kearny, November 11, 1866, NARS, RG 98.

[30] Bisbee, Wands, and Powell, cited above, note 27; General Order Number 41, Headquarters, Fort Philip Kearny, November 18, 1866, NARS, RG 98.

[31] Special Order Number 85, Headquarters, Fort Philip Kearny, December 8, 1866, NARS, RG 98.

[32] Analysis of all official record data on fights.

[33] Henry B. Carrington, comments in Sen. Exec. Doc. 33, 50th Cong., 1st Sess., p. 22.

[34] Henry B. Carrington to Adjutant General, Department of the Platte, November 24, 1866, NARS, RG 98, LR, Department of the Platte; Henry B. Carrington to Adjutant General, Department of the Platte, November 14, 1866, NARS, RG 98, LR, Department of the Platte; telegram, Henry B. Carrington to Adjutant General, Department of the Platte, November 25, 1866, NARS, RG 98, LR, Department of the Platte.

because of poor organization. Captain William J. Fetterman, with a company of mounted infantry, Lieutenant H. S. Bingham, with Company C, 2nd Cavalry, and a small mounted infantry force under Colonel Carrington attempted to pursue and cut off the Indians, in a poorly co-ordinated operation. The three separate groups of soldiers reunited just in time to face about three hundred Indians. Lieutenant Bingham and Sergeant Gideon Bowers were killed, and the rest of the force had a narrow escape. This conflict at last taught *some* of the officers the folly of their often repeated pursuits of Indian parties.[35]

The Sioux, too, learned something from these pursuits. They saw that the troops could be led beyond their artillery support and that a well-co-ordinated decoy-ambush plan might have a chance to succeed. Within two weeks of the Bingham fight, they recruited sufficient manpower from the Sioux and Cheyenne winter camps along the Tongue River and neighboring streams. They laid their plans with uncommon care, even staging a rehearsal. On the morning of December 21, a small party feinted at a wood train several miles west of the fort. Captain Fetterman was sent out with a mixed force of cavalry and infantry to relieve it. He followed the Indian decoys north over Lodgetrail Ridge, and into the deadliest trap ever laid by Indians on the northern Plains. His eighty-man force was overrun in minutes by nearly two thousand Sioux and Cheyenne warriors.[36] Fetterman and his force were killed to a man, but they did inflict substantial casualties on the Indians. Some Crows who saw the fight and other Crows who later talked to some of the participants made estimates ranging from sixteen to one hundred Indians killed, and some summed it up as one hundred killed or dead of wounds.[37]

This was the record disaster of Indian fighting in the West up to the time. Carrington and his garrison were understandably frightened, but they were still in a fairly secure position. There were well over three

[35] Telegram, Henry B. Carrington to Adjutant General, Department of the Platte, December 8, 1866, NARS, RG 98, LR, Department of the Platte; Henry B. Carrington to Adjutant General, Department of the Platte, December 6, 1866, NARS, RG 98, LR, Department of the Platte.

[36] Sen. Exec. Doc. 13, 40th Cong., 1st Sess.; Henry B. Carrington to Adjutant General, Department of the Platte, January 3, 1867, NARS, RG 98, LR, Department of the Platte; Carrington, comments in Sen. Exec. Doc. 33, 50th Cong., 1st Sess., pp. 39–49; "Proceedings of a Court of Inquiry re: the Fetterman Massacre"; George Bird Grinnell, *Fighting Cheyennes* (Norman: University of Oklahoma Press, 1956).

[37] Half Yellow Face, comments in James F. Bradley, "Bradley Manuscript," Book F, *Montana Historical Society Collections*, VIII (1917), 223; Commanding Officer, Fort C.F. Smith, to Adjutant General, Department of the Platte, February 9, 1867, NARS, RG 98, LR, Department of the Platte.

hundred soldiers, one hundred and nineteen male citizen employees of the government,[38] and about fifty other civilians at the post. They had more good small arms and certainly more ammunition than all the Indians in the camps along the Tongue. Four good artillery pieces and abundant ammunition covered all approaches to the fort. They were nearly out of forage, but there was sufficient food, although it was of low quality. Experienced westerners at the fort knew that the Indians had had enough fighting for the present, and would go back to their camps for the winter. The garrison was thus in a sound defensive position.

Carrington, careworn, fatigued, and shocked by the bloody events of the day, penned a hasty dispatch:

Do send me reenforcements forthwith. Expedition now with my force is impossible. I risk everything but the post and its stores. I venture as much as any one can, I have had but today a fight unexampled in Indian warfare; my loss is 94 killed.

I have recovered 49 bodies, and 35 more are to be brought in, in the morning, that have been found. Among the killed are Brevet Lieutenant Colonel Fetterman, Captain F. H. Brown, and Lieutenant Grummond. The Indians engaged were nearly 3,000, being apparently the force reported as on Tongue River, in my dispatches of 5th November and subsequent thereto. This line is important, can and must be held. It will take four times the force in the spring to reopen it, if it be broken up this winter. I hear nothing of my arms that left Leavenworth September 10. The additional cavalry ordered to join me has not been reported; their arrival would have saved us much loss today.

The Indians lost beyond all precedent. I need prompt reenforcement, and repeating arms. I am sure to have, as before reported, an active winter, and must have men and arms. Every officer of this battalion should join it. Today I have every teamster on duty, and but 119 men left at post. I hardly need urge this matter; it speaks for itself. Give me 2 companies of cavalry, at least forthwith, well armed, or 4 companies of infantry, exclusive of what is needed at Reno and Fort Smith.

I did not overestimate my early application of a single company. Promptness will save the line, but our killed shows that any remissness will result in mutilation and butchery beyond precedent. No such mutilation as that today is on record. Depend upon it that the post will be held so long as a round or a man is left. Promptness is the vital thing. Give me officers and men. Only the new Spencer arms should be sent; the Indians are desperate; I spare none, and they spare none.[39]

[38] Post Return for December, 1866, Fort Philip Kearny, NARS, RG 98.

[39] Telegram, Carrington to Adjutant General, Department of the Platte, December 21, 1866, NARS, RG 98, LR, Department of the Platte; telegram, Henry B. Carrington to General Grant, December 21, 1866, NARS, RG 94, LR, Adjutant General's Office.

Four days later, Carrington's two civilian couriers, Daniel Dixon and John "Portugee" Phillips, sent Carrington's message to Omaha from Horseshoe Station.[40] Phillips, carrying a message from Colonel Wessells at Fort Reno to Colonel Palmer at Fort Laramie, rode on to the latter post, and thus into Wyoming legend.[41]

General Philip St. George Cooke, receiving the telegram must, like this writer, have found only two possible interpretations to its contents. Either Carrington was in a state of panic and really believed his whole command to be in danger, or else he was using the first news of the disaster to justify re-enforcements for a massive winter campaign against the hostile Indian camps, a move for which there was not the manpower, the money, and for which there was day by day less military and political support. In either case Carrington's usefulness was at an end.

Cooke did not have to take any summary action against Carrington. He was already on the way out, having himself laid the groundwork for a transfer on July 30, 1866, when he requested command of the 1st Battalion, 18th Infantry, which would remain the 18th Infantry when reorganization went into effect.[42] (The Adjutant General's Office had set up a plan whereby the 1st Battalion would remain the 18th Infantry, the 2nd Battalion would become the 27th Infantry, and the 3rd Battalion would become the 36th Infantry.[43] Carrington was aware of this in September.)[44] On December 21, Headquarters, 1st Battalion, was ordered to Fort Caspar, where Headquarters, 18th Infantry, was to be.[45] Cooke had only to let the routine orders be issued, and Carrington would leave the Mountain District to join his regiment, taking headquarters papers and books with him. These orders went out no later than December 26. Carrington asserted that

[40] Henry B. Carrington, comments in Sen. Exec. Doc. 33, 50th Cong., 1st Sess., p. 44; Lists of Persons and Property Hired, Fort Philip Kearny, December, 1866, NARS, RG 98.

[41] John C. Friend, letter, quoted in Hebard and Brininstool, *Bozeman Trail*, I, 316; telegram, Colonel I. N. Palmer, Fort Laramie, to General Cooke, Omaha, December 26, 1866, NARS, RG 98, LR, TR, Department of the Platte.

[42] Henry B. Carrington to Adjutant General, Department of the Platte, July 30, 1866, NARS, RG 98, LR, Department of the Platte.

[43] A. B. Ostrander, *The Bozeman Trail Forts Under General Philip St. George Cooke* (Seattle, Wash.: privately printed, 1932). Ostrander's account is corroborated by orders and correspondence this writer has examined in NARS, RG 98, Department of the Platte.

[44] Henry B. Carrington, comments in Sen. Exec. Doc. 33, 50th Cong., 1st Sess., pp. 30–31.

[45] Special Order Number 123, Headquarters, Department of the Platte, December 21, 1866, NARS, RG 98.

they had been written and signed before the actual news of the Fetterman fight reached Omaha,[46] but the public, the press, and numerous historians believed what Carrington feared they would believe, that he was removed from command—an obvious untruth,[47] for both a Special Indian Commission and a military Court of Inquiry cleared Carrington in the spring of 1867 of any blame in the Fetterman affair. However, the record of the Court of Inquiry abundantly confirms the lack of training, discipline, and morale in his command.[48] General Philip St. George Cooke summed up Carrington quite fairly when he said: "Colonel Carrington is very plausable [*sic*]—an energetic, industrious man in garrison; but it is too evident that he has not maintained discipline, and that his officers have no confidence in him."[49]

Operations—Wessells, January, 1867–July, 1867

The first arrivals at Fort Philip Kearny after the Fetterman fight were Captain (Brevet Brigadier General) George B. Dandy, Acting Quartermaster, with Lieutenant Alpheus H. Bowman, eighteen men from Fort Reno, and two men en route from Fort C. F. Smith.[50] They came on December 27. Dandy settled quickly into his job as post quartermaster, and assumed the office of District Quartermaster with the reactivation of the Mountain District on January 1, 1867.[51]

Lieutenant Colonel Henry W. Wessells, 18th Infantry, then at Fort Reno, was ordered by General Cooke to move to Fort Philip Kearny and take command of the Mountain District and Fort Philip Kearny at his brevet rank of brigadier general.[52] Cooke ordered two companies of the 2nd Cavalry and four companies of the 18th Infantry to

[46] Henry B. Carrington, comments in Sen. Exec. Doc. 33, 50th Cong., 1st Sess.

[47] Ostrander, *The Bozeman Trail Forts Under General Philip St. George Cooke.*

[48] Sen. Exec. Doc. 13, 40th Cong., 1st Sess., "Proceedings of a Court of Inquiry re: the Fetterman Massacre."

[49] Philip St. George Cooke to General J. A. Rawlins, Chief of Staff, Washington, D.C., December 27, 1866, NARS, RG 98, LS, Department of the Platte.

[50] Record of Events, Post Return for December, 1866, Fort Philip Kearny, NARS, RG 98.

[51] Special Order Number 94, Headquarters, Fort Philip Kearny, December 28, 1866, NARS, RG 98.

[52] Telegram, Philip St. George Cooke to John A. Rawlins, Chief of Staff, December 26, 1866, NARS, RG 94, LR, Adjutant General's Office; telegram, Brevet Brigadier General C. B. Comstock, aide-de-campe to Grant, to Philip St. George Cooke, December 26, 1866, NARS, RG 94, LR, Adjutant General's Office.

report to Wessells at Fort Reno.[53] These re-enforcements were commanded by Major James Van Voast. One of the companies was to stay at Fort Reno and the other five were to accompany Wessells to Fort Philip Kearny.[54] Wessells assumed his new command on January 18, 1867.[55]

The arrival of Wessells and Van Voast with their forces numerically re-enforced Fort Philip Kearny substantially. The net increase in the garrison over its peak December strength was 275, bringing the force to eighteen officers and 657 men.[56] This was at a post General Hazen had recommended as a station for two companies! The re-enforcements posed a serious problem of food and forage, since they had brought none along. Within the month the stock was starving and the men were eating flour and bacon left over by the Connor column. This re-enforcement of Fort Philip Kearny was without doubt the worst move Cooke made. The garrison was already large enough in December, yet the re-enforcements did not make it large enough for campaigning, and thus only worked a hardship on all concerned. In spite of this, the stability, energy, and resourcefulness of Wessells and his staff provided a much-needed stimulus to the command in the dark, cold months of early 1867.

Wessells was a capable and practical man. He did his own work as district and post commander well, and he did not interfere with his subordinates unnecessarily. A very different sort of person from Carrington, he had had over thirty-three years' service as an officer in the regular army at this time, serving with distinction in both the Mexican War and the Civil War.[57] Mrs. Carrington described him as "a gentleman without blemish."[58]

The new arrivals at the fort set to work immediately. Captain Dandy's quartermaster details not only kept the post supplied with

[53] Special Order Number 126, Headquarters, Department of the Platte, December 26, 1866, NARS, RG 98.

[54] Special Order Number 3, Headquarters, Fort Reno, January 10, 1867, NARS, RG 98; General Order Number 1, Headquarters, Fort Reno, January 13, 1867, NARS, RG 98; Post Return for January, 1867, Fort Philip Kearny, NARS, RG 98.

[55] General Order Number 4, Headquarters, Fort Philip Kearny, January 18, 1867, NARS, RG 98.

[56] Post Return for December, 1866, and January, 1867, Fort Philip Kearny, NARS, RG 98.

[57] Francis B. Heitman, *Historical Register and Dictionary of the U.S. Army, 1789–1903* (Washington: Government Printing Office, 1903); *Register of Graduates and Former Cadets of the United States Military Academy* (West Point: United States Military Academy, 1965), p. 219.

[58] Margaret Carrington, *Absaraka*, p. 256.

fuel, but brought in cottonwood tops for forage,[59] and pine tops, at the surgeon's request, for medicinal use.[60] They resumed timber-cutting operations and construction work. By late February they had substantially closed in the fifth and sixth barracks, had built Dandy a fine new quartermaster's office, and had added another large quarter-master's building. Through the spring, they built the shell of the new hospital, and began to upgrade existing structures.[61]

One of Wessells' first concerns was communication with Fort C. F. Smith. Five military parties set out in that direction in January, but all turned back because of deep snow or encounters with the Indians. The trail through the country toward Fort C. F. Smith crossed Goose Creek, Tongue River, and the Little Horn, a few miles above the Indians' favorite wintering sites. A detour into the mountains or any distance onto the Plains would take one into deeper snow country.

Wessells tried to hire civilians to go, but none would make the trip for less than one thousand dollars each. Among the civilians at the post who turned down the chance to go were Robert Bailey, Montgomery Van Valzah, and John "Portugee" Phillips, all capable and experienced couriers.

But early in February, 1867, Sergeant George Grant, Company E, 18th Infantry, and Sergeant Joseph Graham, Company G, 18th Infantry, volunteered to make the trip. They set out at sunrise on February 4, going as far as the wagon bridge at the Pinery on mules, accompanied by one man who took the mules back to the post. Then they strapped on haversacks and snowshoes and set out along the face of the mountain range, striking the main road again on the morning of the fifth. They trudged over the snow, wandering far from the trail for the best footing, and reached Fort C. F. Smith at four o'clock on the afternoon of February 7. After resting through the eighth and ninth, they set out again on the night of February 9. This time they were accompanied by Mich Bouyer, who was placed in charge of the party. All three rode horses and led a pack mule carrying mail. Early on the afternoon of the tenth, they encountered hostile Indians. Bouyer abandoned the mule and the three men raced away.

[59] Murphy, "Forgotten Battalion," pp. 391–392.

[60] Surgeon Samuel Horton to Post Adjutant, Fort Philip Kearny, March 31, 1867, NARS, RG 98, LR, Fort Philip Kearny; endorsement to above letter by Post Adjutant, April 5, 1867, Communications Register, Fort Philip Kearny, NARS, RG 98.

[61] See Chapter 3.

Grant's horse gave out and he fell behind. He killed two of the pursuing Indians and hid out until dark. Graham and Bouyer abandoned their horses, too, and arrived at Fort Philip Kearny ahead of Grant, who came in on the evening of the thirteenth. Strangely, this epic and harrowing walk has had the briefest notice by most historians and has escaped the folklore writers entirely, so these heroes of northern Wyoming remain largely unsung.[62]

With the success of this three-man venture, communications were opened and supply trains passed freely on the road. Wessells and his staff now concentrated as much time as possible on training. First, they set up better controls over assignments to work details, in order to equalize the time spent.[63] They then set up a precise and conventional schedule of calls to time each daily routine.[64] Monthly inspections were made on schedule, starting at the end of January.[65] Management at Fort Reno, generally good after Wessells arrived there in 1866, remained satisfactory.[66] At Fort Philip Kearny, garrison courts-martial provided regular support for discipline.[67] Intensive training started in March. On March 5, Wessells announced a daily recitation in tactics for officers, and schools of instruction for

[62] Sergeant George Grant, Company E, 18th Infantry, to First Lieutenant Thomas L. Brent, commanding Company E, and also to Acting Adjutant General, Mountain District, February 14, 1867, NARS, RG 98, LR, Fort Philip Kearny; Henry W. Wessells, commanding the Mountain District, to Adjutant General, Department of the Platte, February 14, 1867, NARS, RG 98, LR, Department of the Platte; Record of Events, Post Return for February, 1867, Fort Philip Kearny, NARS, RG 98; Record of Events, Post Return for February, 1867, Fort C.F. Smith, NARS, RG 98; Commanding Officer, Fort C.F. Smith, to Adjutant General, Department of the Platte, February 9, 1867, NARS, RG 98, LR, Department of the Platte; Murphy, "Forgotten Battalion," p. 392; William Beckley, "late Company G, 18th Infantry," to Editor George W. Webb, St. Louis, published in the May, 1925, edition of *Winners of the West*; E. S. Topping, *Chronicles of the Yellowstone* (St. Paul: St. Paul Pioneer Press, 1888), p. 56; First Lieutenant Thomas L. Brent, 18th Infantry, quoted in William A. Ganoe, *History of the U.S. Army* (New York: Appleton, 1932); F. M. Fessenden, "Personal Experiences in and around Fort Phil Kearny," in Hebard and Brininstool, *Bozeman Trail*, II; W. F. Beyer and O. F. Keydel, *Deeds of Valor* (Detroit: Perrien-Keydel Co., 1905).

[63] General Order Number 5, Headquarters, Fort Philip Kearny, January 20, 1867, NARS, RG 98.

[64] General Order Number 8, Headquarters, Fort Philip Kearny, January 28, 1867, NARS, RG 98.

[65] General Order Number 9, Headquarters, Fort Philip Kearny, January 29, 1867, NARS, RG 98.

[66] Circular Number 1, Headquarters, Fort Reno, January 30, 1867, NARS, RG 98; Special Order Number 9, Headquarters, Fort Reno, January 30, 1867, NARS, RG 98; General Order Number 3, Headquarters, Fort Reno, January 30, 1867, NARS, RG 98.

[67] Special Order Number 11, Headquarters, Fort Reno, February 3, 1867, NARS, RG 98.

non-commissioned officers.[68] Target practice started the last week in March, with only the men on guard, the sick, and the hospital attendants excused.[69] By mid-April the "school of the soldier" and the "school of the company" were scheduled daily from seven to eight o'clock in the morning and from three to four thirty in the afternoon.[70]

The training was needed, for hostilities began early. Fort Reno lost three men from a hunting party in a fight with the Indians on February 27.[71] On April 2, another unsung hero of the Bozeman Trail was killed. Montgomery Van Valzah, most frequent mail carrier through the previous fall and winter, was returning from Bridgers Ferry with four other citizens en route to Fort Reno and Fort Philip Kearny, when Indians overran and killed the whole party on the Dry Fork of Powder River.[72]

Later the same month, Indians struck as far south as the Platte. Van Voast and a small escort, headed down country as a member of the Carrington Court of Inquiry, beat off a hostile attack on April 20.[73] On April 26 and 27 there were skirmishes with small parties near Fort Reno, and one soldier was killed.[74]

Around Fort Philip Kearny it was quiet until May 16, when Indians drove off twenty-four head of government stock. On May 21 they ran off two horses of Company D, 2nd Cavalry.[75] Visiting Crow Indians lost twenty-five ponies to Sioux raiders on May 25.[76]

But the situation improved with better organization of stock herding,[77] and more experience and training for the men. Sioux

[68] General Order Number 21, Headquarters, Fort Philip Kearny, March 5, 1867, NARS, RG 98.

[69] General Order Number 23, Headquarters, Fort Philip Kearny, March 25, 1867, NARS, RG 98.

[70] General Order Number 28, Headquarters, Fort Philip Kearny, April 14, 1867, NARS, RG 98.

[71] George W. Webb, *Chronological List of Engagements Between the Regular Army of the U.S. and Various Tribes of Hostile Indians which Occurred Between 1790–1890* (St. Joseph, N.J.: Wing Printing Company, 1939); Special Order Number 3, Headquarters, Fort Reno, April 9, 1867, NARS, RG 98.

[72] Proctor, Fort Reno, to Adjutant General, Department of the Platte, April 8, 1867, NARS, RG 98, LR, Department of the Platte; Lieutenant Colonel I. N. Palmer, Commanding Officer, Fort Laramie, to Adjutant General, Department of the Platte, May 11, 1867, NARS, RG 98, LR, Department of the Platte.

[73] Special Order Number 25, Headquarters, Fort Reno, May 10, 1867, NARS, RG 98.

[74] Record of Events, Post Return for May, 1867, Fort Philip Kearny, NARS, RG 98.

[75] Communications Register, Fort Philip Kearny, May 21, 1867, NARS, RG 98.

[76] Record of Events, Post Return for May, 1867, Fort Philip Kearny, NARS, RG 98.

[77] General Order Number 11, Headquarters, Fort Philip Kearny, January 30, 1867, NARS, RG 98.

stock raids on June 2, June 12, and June 18 yielded nothing.[78] They did kill one enlisted herder on May 30 near Fort Reno, but got no stock.[79] Small parties still had to exercise caution, and a hunting party of three soldiers out from Fort Philip Kearny lost one man on June 11.[80]

Friendly Crows became frequent visitors at Fort Philip Kearny in the spring of 1867, adding much color to the scene. From the end of March on, they came in growing numbers, camping along the Piney north and northeast of the fort. John Fitch Kinney, Special Indian Commission member, was there to negotiate with them. His liberal presents and generous promises lured larger numbers, and on June 22 "a large village of Crow Indians came in and camped opposite to the post. They consisted of 118 lodges of Crows and 7 lodges of Nez Perces."[81]

The following day, while Kinney talked to the Crows, a Sioux war party stampeded twenty-five of their horses. The Crow men swept off in hot pursuit, killing three Sioux and returning with nearly all their stock. While they chased the Sioux, Wessells threw out a screen of cavalry pickets beyond the Crow village, with a supporting infantry column to guard the village until the Crow warriors returned. This is almost certainly the incident pictured by Nicolai on Figure 18.[82]

Private William Murphy, observant and critical of the Crows, noted that there were almost always a few of them camped nearby from June on.[83] Soldiers and civilians traded with them.[84] Resourceful troops short of money found them naive at first and on May 16, Wessells issued the following order:

Some thoughtless persons have furnished the friendly Indians in this vicinity with Ceggar papers which are taken by them in good faith. This pernicious practice must be discontinued.[85]

[78] Record of Events, Post Return for June, 1867, Fort Philip Kearny, NARS, RG 98.

[79] Webb, *Chronological List of Engagements Between the Regular Army of the U.S.*

[80] Record of Events, Post Return for June, 1867, Fort Philip Kearny, NARS, RG 98.

[81] *Ibid.*

[82] *Ibid.*; Henry W. Wessells, Fort Philip Kearny, to Adjutant General, Department of the Platte, June 23, 1867, NARS, RG 98, LR, Department of the Platte; J. F. Kinney to Commissioner of Indian Affairs, June 4 and June 17, 1867, Sen. Exec. Doc. 13, 40th Cong., 1st Sess.

[83] Murphy, "Forgotten Battalion," pp. 395–397.

[84] *Ibid.*; Ostrander, *Army Boy of the Sixties*, pp. 198–200.

[85] General Order Number 37, Headquarters, Fort Philip Kearny, May 16, 1867, NARS, RG 98.

A few days later Wessells prohibited selling or bartering with the Indians for any subsistence stores.[86]

For two men the Indian life proved irresistible and they deserted in the company of a band of Crows on May 9, "painted and dressed in Indian costume."[87] One of these, Private Bernard Bravo, Company E, 27th Infantry, lived out his life among the Crows, and served as an interpreter for Lieutenant James Bradley in the 1876 campaign.[88]

Wessells' brief but effective administration of the Mountain District ended early in July, 1867. Brevet Major General John E. Smith, Colonel, 27th Infantry, returned from leave in the spring of 1867. He organized supply trains, recruits, and newly reported officers at North Platte, Nebraska, and marched up country, arriving at Fort Reno on June 29 and at Fort Philip Kearny on July 3.[89] Wessells moved to Fort McPherson, now headquarters post of the 18th Infantry, to act in command of that regiment while Colonel Carrington took a six months leave of absence.[90]

OPERATIONS—SMITH, JULY, 1867–JULY, 1868

Colonel John Eugene Smith, 27th Infantry, was one of those real "discoveries" as an effective troop commander who occasionally turned up in the Civil War volunteer army. Commissioned a colonel in the 45th Illinois Volunteer Infantry in 1861, Smith served most of the war as a brigadier general of volunteers. He received a number of brevets, the highest as Brevet Major General of Volunteers for gallant and meritorious service in action at Savannah.[91]

General Sherman, commanding the Military Division of the Missouri, had held forth hope of a spring campaign through much of Wessells' tenure, but the harsh realities of supply and training delayed a move until a time when the army had its hands full chasing Indians on

[86] General Order Number 38, Headquarters, Fort Philip Kearny, May 21, 1867, NARS, RG 98.

[87] Record of Events, Post Return for May, 1867, Fort Philip Kearny, NARS, RG 98; Communications Register, Fort Philip Kearny, May 20, 1867, NARS, RG 98.

[88] Thomas LeForge, *A White Crow Indian*, ed. Thomas Marquis (New York: Century Company, 1928), pp. 228–232; Edgar I. Stewart, *Custer's Luck* (Norman: University of Oklahoma Press, 1956), pp. 108, 118, 144, 150, 158, 299.

[89] Wishart, "Diary," covers this period well.

[90] Monthly Rosters, Distribution of Troops in the Department of the Platte, 1867, NARS, RG 94.

[91] Heitman, *Historical Register and Dictionary*.

the Kansas frontier and protecting the high-priority rail construction crews. Then, before Colonel Smith had barely settled at Fort Philip Kearny, a new peace commission was appointed, with Sherman as a member.[92] No one really wanted to expend the resources for a big campaign to ensure safety on the Bozeman Trail, for it would soon be obsolete. Yet there was still some travel on it, and troops would have to remain there until the railroad cut off travel substantially. This meant another year of limited warfare.

Colonel Smith assumed command of the Mountain District and Fort Philip Kearny on July 5, 1867.[93] He had a strong staff. His assistant was Major Benjamin F. Smith, 27th Infantry, a seasoned regular with a distinguished Civil War record. (Major Smith held a brevet of Brigadier General of Volunteers, and some writers have confused the two Smiths.)[94]

Major James Van Voast, 18th Infantry, returned to the Mountain District and took command of Fort Reno, now garrisoned by men of the 18th Infantry, leaving the troops of the 27th Infantry concentrated at Fort Philip Kearny.[95]

Colonel Smith sent Lieutenant Colonel L. P. Bradley, 27th Infantry, with re-enforcements, recruits, and supplies, to take command of Fort C. F. Smith.[96] Bradley, another Civil War volunteer turned regular, had a fine record, and a brevet of Brigadier General.[97]

Smith's supply trains carried a new Model 1866 Springfield breech-loading rifle musket for each infantryman in the District, and an adequate reserve of ammunition. There were two hundred shiny, copper-cased .50–70 caliber cartridges to the rifle, "Martin's Bar Anvil Primed."[98] As a Fourth of July celebration, the ever practical Van Voast had the Fort Reno garrison practice with their new weapons and with the mountain howitzer.[99]

[92] Robert G. Athearn, *William Tecumseh Sherman and the Settlement of the West* (Norman: University of Oklahoma Press, 1956).
[93] General Order Number 47, Headquarters, Fort Philip Kearny, July 5, 1867, NARS, RG 98; Record of Events, Post Return for July, 1867, Fort Philip Kearny, NARS, RG 98.
[94] Heitman, *Historical Register and Dictionary.*
[95] General Order Number 18, Headquarters, Fort Reno, June 30, 1867, NARS, RG 98.
[96] Special Order Number 110, Headquarters, Fort Philip Kearny, July 9, 1867, NARS, RG 98; Record of Events, Post Return for July, 1867, Fort Philip Kearny, NARS, RG 98.
[97] Heitman, *Historical Register and Dictionary.*
[98] See "Arms and Ammunition," Chapter 4.
[99] General Order Number 21, Headquarters, Fort Reno, July 3, 1867, NARS, RG 98.

Reorganization of the District and preparations for Bradley's march to Fort C. F. Smith consumed much time at Fort Philip Kearny. Routine activities including drill were held, but there is no evidence that target practice began until early August.[100]

On the morning of July 5—the day Smith took command—between twenty and thirty Indians scouted Smith's camp below the post, but withdrew when pickets gave an alarm.[101] They struck next on the twelfth, taking only two horses. Company D, 2nd Cavalry, pursued them a short distance, unsuccessfully.[102]

Colonel Smith placed Major Benjamin F. Smith in charge of all training activities at the post on July 13. In the same order he set forth new rules for the wood-train escort:

> The officer in charge will exercise the greatest vigilance in the protection of the train and stock against sudden dashes of Indians and in the event of him being attacked he will merely act on the defensive and will not pursue the enemy nor go beyond the protection of his train. The men will be supplied with 40 rounds of ammunition per man.[103]

Van Voast tightened Fort Reno's defensive management at about this time, also:

> Hereafter, when an alarm of Indians or of fire is given by the sentinel on post the men will at once repair to their respective company grounds and await orders. The practice of running outside, climbing upon quarters, bastions or stockade is in direct violation of orders and the sentinels are instructed to fire upon anyone so doing.[104]

One hundred and fifty Indians tried to stampede the herds near Fort Philip Kearny on July 16, without success.[105] The next day the herders repulsed another such attempt.[106] These raids led Smith to further prescribe precautions to be taken against such attacks:

> To guard against successful dashes of hostile Indians in running off stock in the vicinity of the post and that prompt and efficient aid may be ready to reinforce the herders:

[100] Wishart, "Diary," July entries; Special Order Number 104, Headquarters, Fort Philip Kearny, July 3, 1867, NARS, RG 98; General Order Number 49, Headquarters, Fort Philip Kearny, July 7, 1867, NARS, RG 98; Special Order Number 110, Headquarters, Fort Philip Kearny, July 9, 1867, NARS, RG 98.

[101] Wishart, "Diary," July 5, 1867.

[102] *Ibid.,* July 12, 1867; Record of Events, Post Return for July, 1867, Fort Philip Kearny, NARS, RG 98.

[103] Special Order Number 113, Headquarters, Fort Philip Kearny, July 13, 1867, NARS, RG 98.

[104] General Order Number 23, Headquarters, Fort Reno, July 15, 1867, NARS, RG 98.

[105] Wishart, "Diary," July 16, 1867.

[106] Record of Events, Post Return for July, 1867, Fort Philip Kearny, NARS, RG 98.

A. Co. 27th Infty is hereby designated for one week when it will be relieved by another company, to hold itself in readiness to move in double-quick time by the nearest route to the protection of the herd.

The signal of Indians from the picket hill will be sufficient authority under this order for the company to fall in and move out under the officer present.

D. Co., 2d U.S. Cavalry in grazing its animals will always go out for that purpose with at least 15 saddled horses and in the event of an attack upon any of the herds will render prompt assistance, at the same time driving in their own stock.

This order will not be construed to authorize the company to go beyond the line of hills or out of support of the garrison.

The troops at this post will have habitually forty rounds of ammunition in their cartridge boxes. Company commanders are held responsible that this paragraph is complied with.[107]

The Indians tried to stampede contractor's stock at the Pinery on July 19, but were again unsuccessful.[108]

Throughout this entire period of hostile activity, both Smith and Van Voast had intensive construction and repair work under way, and committed substantial portions of their garrisons to escort duty.[109]

Just at this time the Sioux launched their second and last concerted effort in the Bozeman Trail country. Brought together by the Sun Dance, they launched two massive war parties when the ceremonies were over. Possibly over five hundred warriors headed for Fort C. F. Smith, and about a thousand gathered above Fort Philip Kearny. The Indians at Fort C. F. Smith harassed a small party of hay cutters and their escort for about three hours on August 1. In the ensuing fight, the twenty-seven defenders of the "hay corral" had three of their men killed and three wounded, and an estimated eight Indians killed and as many as thirty more wounded.[110]

The contingent around Fort Philip Kearny attacked thirty-two defenders of the wood camp in the famous Wagon Box fight. After several unsuccessful attempts to overrun the position, the Indians withdrew and milled about out of range until driven off by a relief party from the fort under Major Benjamin F. Smith. Smith dispersed the Indians with a single air-burst, twelve-pounder spherical case

[107] Special Order Number 117, Headquarters, Fort Philip Kearny, July 18, 1867, NARS, RG 98.

[108] Record of Events, Post Return for July, 1867, Fort Philip Kearny, NARS, RG 98.

[109] Much of the Special Orders sequence of both posts is devoted to these activities.

[110] Record of Events, Post Return for August, 1867, Fort C.F. Smith, NARS, RG 98.

from his howitzer. Captain Powell estimated that sixty Indians were killed and one hundred and twenty were wounded. Since the troops were not yet familiar with their new rifles, and the Indians would retreat rather than suffer heavy casualties, this figure is probably a maximum. At any rate, the Sioux lost their enthusiasm for a big fight. It seems significant that the Oglallas and several other Sioux tribes did not again deliberately bring any considerable body of their people against troops until June 17, 1876, on the Rosebud.

But the real significance of the Wagon Box fight and the Hay Field fight was the impact on troop morale. The men now realized that organization, discipline, reasonable alertness, and good weapons, well employed, gave them command of the situation. The Indian was henceforth not a superhuman enemy, but merely another dangerous predator.[111]

Colonel Smith and Major Van Voast moved supply trains, forage and wood trains, and other parties through the ensuing months with these same small forces, usually of less than thirty men, occasionally of company strength.[112] Sometimes they took along a mountain howitzer. Captain H. B. Freeman's company-strength wagon-train escort was jumped by a large Sioux force near Connor's Springs on August 13, 1867, and three men were wounded. The howitzer drove the Indians off.[113] Lieutenant F. F. Whitehead with less than a company routed Indian attackers while in the field near Fort Reno the next day. The Sioux did kill two civilian herders on August 16 out from Fort Reno, but got no stock.[114]

Small parties camping at the Pinery or with the haying parties usually built a field fortification in this period. Lieutenant Alexander Wishart noted that his force made a wagon-bed corral and threw up an earthwork against it on August 6 and 7. A few Indians reconnoitered the position on the eighth from the hills, but drew off after

[111] *Ibid.*; "Report of Captain James Powell on the Engagement with the Indians, August 2, 1867," NARS, RG 98, LR, Department of the Platte; "Report of the Relief Expedition, August 2, 1867," by Major Benjamin F. Smith, NARS, RG 98, LR, Department of the Platte; Wishart, "Diary," August 3, 1867.

[112] Special Order Number 130, Headquarters, Fort Philip Kearny, August 5, 1867, NARS, RG 98; Special Order Number 131, Headquarters, Fort Philip Kearny, August 6, 1867, NARS, RG 98; Wishart, "Diary," August 6–13, 1867; Special Order Number 63, Headquarters, Fort Reno, August 7, 1867, NARS, RG 98; Special Order Number 134, Headquarters, Fort Philip Kearny, August 12, 1867, NARS, RG 98; Special Order Number 66, Headquarters, Fort Reno, August 13, 1867, NARS, RG 98.

[113] Captain Henry B. Freeman, "Report of an Engagement with Indians while on Escort Duty to Fort Reno," submitted at Fort Philip Kearny, August 18, 1867, NARS, RG 98, LR, Department of the Platte.

[114] Webb, *Chronological List of Engagements.*

seeing the earthwork.[115] At a hay ground on September 4, the troops built a large dugout, roofed with timber, apparently rather like the "monitors" along the railroad lines in the same year.[116] Hay cutters near Fort Reno also fortified their camps.[117] Through this same period training was intensified, and informal target practice near the posts was encouraged at specified hours of the day.[118] Men at the Pinery felt secure enough to hunt, and their success with the new .50–70's brought a welcome change of diet.[119]

Indian activity diminished for several months to ordinary stock raids. The largest of these is an interesting study of one of the few instances of Indian success that fall.

Lieutenant Ephraim Tillotson, 27th Infantry, with twenty men, took over guard of a hay camp on the Piney on the evening of September 21. They threw up a sod breastwork at the camp site. Just at the end of the dinner hour the next day, the picket on a nearby hill gave the signal for Indians. About thirty mounted Indians had sneaked up under cover of brush along the Piney and burst from cover at a gallop, trying to drive off the mule herd. Troops and part of the dozen citizen hay cutters ran into the earthwork and opened fire. All but one Indian from this party swung away and swept through the herd of oxen, shooting arrows at them. The lone Indian kept on with those mules and horses that would run, braving a heavy but ineffective fire. Another party of twenty Indians swept out from behind a hill and tried to cut off the picket who was coming down from his guard post. He stopped and fired at them, backed up by the troops in the earthwork. At this, the Indians broke off the engagement and ran away. Sixteen mules and five horses were taken, and one ox was killed and several wounded. All was contractor stock. A board of officers investigated the affair, concluding that the citizens had not hobbled their stock, and that Tillotson had not conducted the defense well, due to inexperience.[120]

[115] Wishart, "Diary," August 6, 7, 8, 1867.
[116] *Ibid.,* September 4 and 5, 1867.
[117] William Beckley, Company G, 18th Infantry, to George W. Webb, editor, *Winners of the West,* May, 1925, p. 3.
[118] General Order Number 55, Headquarters, Fort Philip Kearny, August 8, 1867, NARS, RG 98.
[119] Wishart, "Diary," September 9, 11, and 12, 1867.
[120] Special Order Number 158, Headquarters, Fort Philip Kearny, September 21, 1867, NARS, RG 98; "Proceedings of a Board of Officers at Fort Phil Kearny, September 27, 1867," NARS, RG 98, LR, Department of the Platte; Special Order Number 161, Headquarters, Fort Philip Kearny, September 25, 1867, NARS, RG 98; Wishart, "Diary," September 22, 1867.

Apparently, Colonel Smith felt that policy limited him to defensive operations, and he seemed to feel secure on this basis, for he relieved the excellent guide, Jim Bridger, from duty at the post on September 23, 1867, ending his last western field service. Bridger was ordered to report to the Department commander, thus assuring this grand old mountain man of government transportation as far as Omaha.[121]

Over the next two months there were seven small engagements up and down the line, in which one civilian, two soldiers, and six Indians were killed, and three soldiers and three Indians were wounded.[122] In addition, Captain A. S. Burt with recruits and a wagon train had an hour-long moonlight fire-fight with over fifty Indians while camped on Crazy Woman Fork around two in the morning on November 13, 1867. His force suffered no loss. They would not positively claim any Indians killed, but were "fully convinced that we had hurt somebody."[123] A Wells Fargo contract train without an escort lost one hundred and thirty-two head of oxen on November 18 at Wind Creek.[124]

The last consequential flurry of action of the early period in the Powder River country occurred in December, 1867. On December 2, Sergeant Joseph Graham (one of the trio who had made the trip to Fort C. F. Smith in February) was hunting alone, with permission. As he passed within three quarters of a mile of a grazing beef herd, thirty Indians charged him. He killed two of their horses and held them off until the herders arrived to re-enforce him. Major Van Voast commended him in official orders, saying:

> Sergeant Graham's conduct was witnessed by the officers and many men of the Fort and it is hoped that this example, showing what one person can do, will not be forgotten by any man of this command, if surprised or in the presence of hostile Indians. Sergeant Graham owes his life to his self-possession and to the skilfulness with which he used his breech-loading rifle and his conduct is an additional commendation to that which he already received in General Order No. 26, Headquarters, Department of the Platte, dated Omaha, Nebr., May 25, 1867.[125]

[121] Special Order Number 159, Headquarters, Fort Philip Kearny, September 23, 1867, NARS, RG 98.

[122] Wishart, "Diary," September 24, 1867; Webb, *Chronological List of Engagements.*

[123] Andrew S. Burt, quoted in Merrill J. Mattes, *Indians, Infants, and Infantry* (Denver: Rosenstock, 1960), pp. 118–119.

[124] Deposition of William McPherson, Wagonmaster, Wells-Fargo Contract Train Number 102, given at Fort Philip Kearny, December 8, 1867, NARS, RG 98, LR, Department of the Platte.

[125] General Order Number 36, Fort Reno, December 25, 1867, NARS, RG 98; William Beckley, Company G, 18th Infantry, to George W. Webb, editor, *Winners of the West*, May, 1925, p. 3.

Sergeant Gillaspy and twenty-two men of Company C, 18th Infantry, fought the last sizable engagement in the region the first three days of December when the supply train they were guarding was corralled by sixty Indians a mile above Crazy Woman Crossing. Gillaspy's force and the sixteen citizens of the train built breastworks of sacked grain and potatoes and defended the train successfully until the arrival of Captain D. S. Gordon's Company D, 2nd Cavalry, on December 3. One soldier was killed in this fight, and three enlisted men and four civilians were wounded.[126] Two civilians killed near the Pinery on December 14 appear to be the last casualties of the season.[127]

Three very quiet months followed. Communications were regular, supplies moved as often as weather permitted, and the garrison of each post kept up routine work and training.[128]

In the spring there were only three significant engagements. One was an unsuccessful attack on a mail party on the Dry Fork early in March. The others were the killing of an Indian on Rock Creek by a cavalry patrol on April 3, and in June an incident some distance from Fort Reno in which one man lost his life through carelessness when he strayed away from his party, who drove off the attackers. He was the last casualty of the Bozeman Trail operation.[129]

Grant ordered preparations to abandon the line of posts in telegrams on March 2 and 3, 1868.[130] From this date on, activities moved toward an orderly phase-out of the now obsolete Bozeman Trail operation. Boards of Survey and quartermaster details increased as stores were sorted and packed. Regular training and schedules continued, however.[131]

Troop movements began in June. Major Benjamin F. Smith, with Companies B and F, 27th Infantry, left Fort Philip Kearny and

---

[126] General Order Number 36, Headquarters, Fort Reno, December 25, 1867, NARS, RG 98; Deposition of William McPherson, Wagonmaster, given at Fort Philip Kearny, December 8, 1867, NARS, RG 98, LR, Department of the Platte; Deposition of Captain D. S. Gordon, given at Fort Philip Kearny, December 7, 1867, NARS, RG 98, LR, Department of the Platte.

[127] Webb, *Chronological List of Engagements.*

[128] Survey of post orders and correspondence, both posts.

[129] Van Voast, Fort Reno, to Adjutant General, Mountain District, March 13, 1868, NARS, RG 98, LS, Fort Reno; Webb, *Chronological List of Engagements.*

[130] Telegrams, Grant to Sherman, March 2 and 3, 1868, NARS, RG 94, LR, Adjutant General's Office; Sherman to Augur, March 7, 1868, NARS, RG 98, LR, Department of the Platte.

[131] General Order Number 21, Headquarters, Fort Reno, May 13, 1868, NARS, RG 98.

marched to Fort Reno, taking over that post on June 16.[132] Major Van Voast and the former 18th Infantry garrison of Fort Reno moved down the road out of the country the next day.[133]

Captain A. S. Burt and Companies I and D, 27th Infantry, were ordered down from Fort C. F. Smith to Fort Philip Kearny.[134]

Troops remaining at Fort Philip Kearny cleaned up the post cemetery and erected a "monument to the memory of the soldiers killed by Indians."[135]

Major Benjamin F. Smith died suddenly at Fort Reno the morning of June 23, and First Lieutenant James McBride Stembel assumed command.[136]

Company D, 2nd Cavalry, left Fort Philip Kearny for Fort Laramie on July 1, 1867.[137] In mid-July, Dr. Horton left for Fort D. A. Russell with medical stores.[138]

The last civilian wagon train up the Bozeman Trail in this period, on its way to Montana, was a John Richard, Jr., outfit, with John Porie (J. B. Pourier, "Big Bat") as wagonmaster. The train left Fort Philip Kearny on July 20, 1868. These case-hardened westerners numbered nineteen men armed with fifteen guns and five hundred rounds of ammunition![139]

Smith sent Captain George M. Templeton with Company D, 27th Infantry, to Fort Reno. He took command of that post on August 1, 1868, relieving First Lieutenant Jacob Paulus, at that time in command.[140]

[132] Special Order Number 63, Headquarters, Fort Philip Kearny, June 9, 1868, NARS, RG 98; Special Order Number 64, Headquarters, Fort Philip Kearny, June 10, 1868, NARS, RG 98; General Order Number 25, Headquarters, Fort Reno, June 15, 1868, NARS, RG 98.

[133] General Order Number 25, Headquarters, Fort Reno, June 15, 1868, NARS, RG 98; General Order Number 26, Headquarters, Fort Reno, June 16, 1868, NARS, RG 98; General Order Number 1, NS, Headquarters, Fort Reno, June 16, 1868, NARS, RG 98.

[134] Special Order Number 63, Headquarters, Fort Philip Kearny, June 9, 1868, NARS, RG 98.

[135] *Ibid.,* Number 66, June 12, 1868.

[136] *Ibid.,* Number 6, June 22, 1868; General Order Number 5, Headquarters, Fort Reno, June 22, 1868, NARS, RG 98.

[137] Special Order Number 77, Headquarters, Fort Philip Kearny, June 30, 1868, NARS, RG 98.

[138] *Ibid.,* Number 83, July 13, 1868.

[139] Wagon Train Book, Fort Philip Kearny, 1868, entry for July 20–23, NARS, RG 98.

[140] Special Order Number 92, Headquarters, Fort Philip Kearny, July 29, 1868, NARS, RG 98; General Order Number 8, Headquarters, Fort Reno, August 1, 1868, NARS, RG 98; General Order Number 9, Headquarters, Fort Reno, August 1, 1868, NARS, RG 98.

Colonel John E. Smith officially abandoned Fort Philip Kearny on August 1, 1868, moving into camp to await transportation. With this he closed the post records.[141] Their bull trains left Fort Reno for Fort Philip Kearny on August 1, so they may well have been at Fort Philip Kearny as late as August 7 or 8, allowing normal time on the road, plus normal loading time for trains of this size.[142] The last available entries in the Fort Reno records are August 11, 1868, and National Archives correspondence points to August 18 as the last departure of troops from that post.[143]

Their departure down the dusty trail ended Colonel Smith's notably successful year of administration of the Mountain District. He was appreciated by his men as "strict but just," and applauded because he ordered routine drill and target practice, and "things went along better."[144] Smith should be ranked as one of the best commanders of the Indian wars. He is, however, among the least truly appreciated, since he provoked no political controversies, received no massed surrenders of starving Indians, and suffered no notorious defeats. He went on to command other posts, such as Fort Laramie, and other regiments. He founded Fort Robinson and Camp Sheridan in Nebraska to guard the restless reservation Sioux.[145] In these later years he did his job, coolly, efficiently, and well, just as he had closed out the unpleasant, limited war in the Powder River country in 1867–1868.

[141] General Order Number 12, Headquarters, Fort Philip Kearny, July 30, 1868, NARS, RG 98.

[142] Special Order Number 24, Headquarters, Fort Reno, August 1, 1868, NARS, RG 98.

[143] General Order Number 10, Headquarters, Fort Reno, August 11, 1868, NARS, RG 98; General Order Number 11, Headquarters, Fort Reno, August 11, 1868, NARS, RG 98; Preliminary Checklist, Records of U.S. Army Commands, 1941, NARS, RG 98.

[144] Murphy, "Forgotten Battalion," pp. 394–398.

[145] Records of the "Sioux Expedition," 1874, NARS, RG 98, LR, Department of the Platte.

Part II

Posts in the Closing Years of the Frontier Army

Chapter 6. Evolution of Policy, 1868–1876

There was little disappointment at the abandonment of the early posts in 1868. They had served their purpose and were no longer needed. The railroad line was pushing rapidly toward completion as Cheyenne, Laramie City, Rock River, Medicine Bow, Benton, and then Rawlins successively became the jumping-off points to the West and to the mines. Some suggested a new line of posts along the Bridger Trail through the dry Big Horn Basin, but General Sherman stated his opposition to such marginal emigrant routes in March, 1868:

> You will note what General Grant says about the new line of posts west of the Big Horn Range. I await your opinion on this matter, but think that no line at all should be planned, and we should keep our troops near the railroad, till it reaches the longitude of Salt Lake, when the road now travelled from there to Montana will become the one in use, and therefore best entitled to military protection. I don't believe in the necessity or policy of banishing our men to that wild mountain region till it is demonstrated to be of some practical use.[1]

Fort D. A. Russell, Fort Sanders, Fort Fred Steele, and a revitalized Fort Bridger were now the main posts, with good railroad transport, fast mail service, and the telegraph; while Fort Laramie, a highly developed post, and the new Fort Fetterman, both only ninety miles from the railroad line, were the important bases from which the army would advance in any role it was called upon to play with the northern Plains tribes.

Fort Ellis and Fort Shaw guarded the gateways to the established mining country in Montana. Along the Missouri River half a dozen

[1] Lieutenant General W. T. Sherman to Brevet Major General C. C. Augur, March 7, 1868, NARS, RG 98, LR, Department of the Platte.

posts guarded the eastern line around the Sioux country.[2] Some Indians may have felt more secure when the troops from Fort Philip Kearny and Fort Reno withdrew, but it was a false security, for they were actually encircled by a ring of steam and steel. As the Sioux settled down to Indian summer, 1868, the army waited, too, for policy to recall its troops to action.

Outside the now enclosed Sioux country the westward-moving frontier was being rapidly closed in and consolidated prior to the final rush of northern Plains settlement. Mining enclaves spread through neighboring valleys; stock raising and farming thrived around the mining towns and filled the valleys with settlements. Northward, over the newly conquered southern Plains, hardy, weathered, and ambitious cattlemen pushed their noisy herds in an increasing stream, to feed the agency Indians and to fill the ranges south of the Sioux country.[3]

Peace policy succeeded as well as could be expected in the growing clouds of scandal surrounding the Grant administration. Such successes as it did enjoy were due mostly to the fact that not enough people wanted the Sioux land badly enough to fight for it—at least not yet! Through all this, the army waited and invested its meager resources in pinching out other Indian settlements, in technical research, and in establishing livable posts along communications and transport routes.[4]

Railroad builders turned to construction of secondary lines and branches, but there was much pressure for alternate transcontinental routes, and the surveyors moved along those routes. One proposal in favor at the time was to build a line west across the prairies of North Dakota to the Yellowstone, following its valley to the easy passes of Montana, and then to the booming Pacific Northwest. Surveys and construction crews proceeded steadily westward toward the Missouri, while other surveying parties moved along the route from west to east, taking on a military escort as they moved down to the Yellowstone in August, 1872. The northern tribes of Sioux, assembled as they often did in midsummer, made a desultory fight with Baker's

[2] Francis Paul Prucha, *Guide to the Military Posts of the United States* (Madison: Wisconsin Historical Society, 1963).

[3] Robert G. Athearn, *High Country Empire* (Lincoln: University of Nebraska Press, 1964); Athearn, *William Tecumseh Sherman and the Settlement of the West* (Norman: University of Oklahoma Press, 1956).

[4] William H. Leckie, *Conquering the Southern Plains* (Norman: University of Oklahoma Press, 1964); *Reports of the Chief of Ordnance* for the large volume of research done in the years 1866–1894.

escort on August 14.[5] This skirmish led the Northern Pacific to secure a heavy escort for their surveyors the next year. The 7th Cavalry, guarding the survey parties, found the northern Sioux tribes belligerent but careful in their several small skirmishes along the Yellowstone.[6]

Financial problems stalled the Northern Pacific that year, but in 1874 mining interests took the field. Active Montana promoters organized the "Yellowstone Wagon Road and Prospecting Expedition"—a catchy title—"Wagon Road" to lure capital, territorial, and governmental support; "Prospecting" to attract manpower from the tough, seasoned citizens of the Gallatin Valley. Another purpose of the expedition may have been to provoke the Indians to a war in which the army would clear the Sioux country for development. Although the prospecting party found no gold, and merely re-established the known fact that the Yellowstone from its head-of-navigation to Bozeman Pass could be traversed by wagons, they did stir up the Indians. With new Montana Militia .50–70's, plenty of ammunition, two artillery pieces, and poisoned bait, they bested the Sioux in a series of fights, and moved freely through the choice Sioux country along the Rosebud and the Big Horn drainage. This re-emphasized the longstanding army contention that citizen parties who took the trouble to organize and arm themselves could pass through Indian country without significant loss.[7]

Rumor had long held out the lure of mineral wealth in the Black Hills along the boundary between the reservation and the unceded Sioux lands. In the summer of 1874, a well-staffed government expedition, with Lieutenant Colonel George A. Custer commanding a strong escort and massive support train, struck straight to the Black Hills, filling in gaps of the early maps of the region, and sent out the word, "Gold at the grass roots!"

Pressure had long been mounting to open up the Sioux country, but gold was the magic word that changed government policy. The Sioux City, Yankton, Bismarck, and Cheyenne newspapers promoted invasion of the Hills. The next spring, miners and mining camp followers by the thousands set out for the Black Hills. Bound by

[5] Stanley Vestal, *New Sources of Indian History* (Norman: University of Oklahoma Press, 1934), pp. 168–170.

[6] Edgar I. Stewart, *Custer's Luck* (Norman: University of Oklahoma Press, 1956), pp. 55–60.

[7] E. S. Topping, *Chronicles of the Yellowstone* (St. Paul: St. Paul Pioneer Press, 1888); W. T. Hamilton, *My Sixty Years on the Plains* (Norman: University of Oklahoma Press, 1962); James S. Hutchins, "Poison in the Pemmican," *Montana*, VIII, Number 3 (Summer 1958).

treaty to keep them out, the government tried, but found that it could not withstand the onslaught of resourceful prospectors, ambitious politicians, promoters, and newsmen, who all conspired to make the army's efforts futile.

In September, 1875, the government attempted to buy from the Indians a mining settlement that had already been overtaken, but even the reservation Sioux would have none of this, and were incensed at the thought of miners tearing up the country they called their "Sacred Blackness."[8]

Nevertheless, white occupation of the Hills was a fact, and the security of its communications and transport routes was now a matter of vital interest to a huge region all around the Sioux country. Even the Peace party grew less effective, as many an unsuccessful reformer, just as a decade and a half earlier on the slavery question, turned to advocacy of the use of force to sell social change to an unwilling client.[9] Westerners saw this as a chance to open up a vast region for development. Taken together the pressures built up fast. Policy officials conferred at the White House in November, and agreed to give an ultimatum to the Sioux.[10]

The story of the next six months has been explored from virtually every angle by a legion of writers, and can be summed up briefly. The Sioux, for various reasons, paid no heed to the ultimatum; and the army responded by planning a three-pronged invasion of the Powder River country, a sort of bigger and better Connor campaign. Brigadier General George Crook made a hasty sortie into the Powder River country in March, 1876, but he succeeded only in committing the Cheyennes to a fight to the last, and in stirring up the Indians generally,[11] for now hundreds of young reservation Sioux joined the others, for "one last big fight."

Colonel John Gibbon guarded the Yellowstone in the spring.[12] Brigadier General Crook assembled a large expedition at Fort Fetter-

[8] Stewart, *Custer's Luck*, pp. 61–65; Harry H. Anderson, "A Challenge to Brown's Sioux Indian Wars Thesis," *Montana*, XII, Number 1 (Winter 1962), 40–49; Senate Executive Document 32, 43rd Cong., 2nd Sess. (reports of the "Black Hills Expedition").

[9] Henry E. Fritz, *The Movement for Indian Assimilation, 1860–1890* (Philadelphia: University of Pennsylvania Press, 1963), pp. 120–134, 171–188.

[10] Anderson, "A Challenge to Brown's Sioux Indian Wars Thesis."

[11] J. W. Vaughn, *Reynolds' Campaign on Powder River* (Norman: University of Oklahoma Press, 1961).

[12] James F. Bradley, in Edgar I. Stewart, ed., *March of the Montana Column* (Norman: University of Oklahoma Press, 1961).

man, and moved off through the next few weeks with comic-opera flair, newspaper reporters tagging along to get in on the fun.[13] Brigadier General Terry's column plodded westward from the Missouri River, its complex cast daily taking on the appearance of a classic tragedy.[14]

The annual summer Sun Dance cleared the spiritual air for the gathering tribes, and warriors from the massive camp set out on a typical post-celebration crusade, seeking Crook's column, of whose presence they were aware. They caught Crook's force unsaddled on the Rosebud and both sides fought to a standstill. Crook gained a new appreciation of the numbers and individual fighting qualities of the Sioux and Cheyennes. The Indians, for their part, found that the white soldier of 1876, if well led, could stand up and fight. Neither side had significant losses, and both thankfully retired from the field, having had their fill of fighting.

The huge Indian camp moved and grew. On one hot June afternoon, Custer blundered into it with his force, as so often, dispersed while searching for Indians. Thus, after ten years, Custer at last found Indians a-plenty, and through them death and lasting fame.

Word of the Custer disaster and other near disasters shocked the nation, and threw even greater support behind the policy to finish the Indian question as a military problem.[15] The new and better-planned campaigns in the fall of 1876 paved the way for the reoccupation of the Powder River country. This time the objective was very different —to break up the Indian's freedom of movement and to harass him at his source of supply, thereby effectively opening up the country for settlement. This, then, is the context in which the Powder River posts functioned after 1876.

[13] Vaughn, *With Crook at the Rosebud* (Harrisburg: Stackpole, 1956).
[14] Stewart, *Custer's Luck*; Fred Dustin, *The Custer Tragedy* (Saginaw, Michigan: Edwards Publishers, 1965).
[15] Sources listed above, notes 10–14, on Summer, 1876, campaigns.

Chapter 7. Structural History of Cantonment Reno (Fort McKinney No. One)

There was no uncertainty about policy in the fall of 1876. The Custer disaster had taken care of that. Crook's mission and that of other commanders was now to seek out and destroy the hostile Indian bands, to make their last-stand country untenable to them, to occupy it, forcing them to go back to the reservations.[1]

An active offensive required sizable and mobile forces. Crook assembled a mixed force from companies of the 2nd, 3rd, 4th, and 5th Cavalry regiments, totaling nearly a whole regiment in strength. This, under Colonel R. S. Mackenzie, would be his mobile striking force. He took along a company-strength force of Pawnee Scouts, and expected to rendezvous with groups of Shoshoni and Crow scouts and irregulars.[2] So that the force might be truly mobile, Crook had to establish supply camps in the hostile country, since wagon transport accompanying a fast-moving column of this kind had a point of diminishing return in its radius of operations. Cantonment Reno was one of these supply bases, established by a four-company force drawn from units of the 4th, 9th, and 23rd Infantry regiments, under command of Captain Edwin Pollock of the 9th Infantry.[3]

[1] Robert G. Athearn, *William Tecumseh Sherman and the Settlement of the West* (Norman: University of Oklahoma Press, 1956); Martin F. Schmitt, editor, comment in *Autobiography of General George Crook* (Norman: University of Oklahoma Press, 1960).

[2] Robert Bruce, *The Fighting Norths and Pawnee Scouts* (Lincoln: Nebraska State Historical Society, 1932), pp. 48–54.

[3] General Order Number 1, Cantonment Reno Series, issued by Pollock while in camp near Fort Fetterman, October 3, 1876; Record of Events, Post Return for October, 1876, Cantonment Reno, NARS, RG 98.

Captain Pollock assumed command of the post, selected a site, and named it on October 14, 1876.[4] Ordered only to establish a base in the vicinity of the old Fort Reno, he chose a spot about three miles upstream. The site is located in the Northeast quarter of Section 17, Township 44 North, Range 78 West, of the 6th Principal Meridian (see Figure 18). It lies on a low stream terrace about five to ten feet above the flood plain, on the left (west) bank of the Powder, within a broad bend of the stream, nearly opposite the mouth of Dry Fork. The location has confused modern travelers for a number of years—including some who should have known better! Army surveys at the time of its occupancy, along with abundant surface evidence, pinpoint the site as that of Cantonment Reno.[5]

There is no indication why Pollock chose this particular area. One might surmise that it was because it was close to water, and had an adequate stretch of level land. As he stayed on there, Pollock became instrumental in securing removal of the post to its later site on the Clear Fork, near Buffalo.[6]

Setting to work with great energy, Pollock and his men built extensively, if not well. Working outward from their tent camp, they first built a storehouse, since supplies were their main concern. They hewed out square timbers from river bottom cottonwoods, bedded sizable cottonwood sills in the ground, and built a "balloon" framework. They covered this with tarpaulins. There is no evidence of the size or the precise location of this warehouse, but it must have been large in view of the quantities of supplies involved and its mode of construction.[7]

Next came two storage cellars for perishable commodities, built side by side, each about twenty by eighty feet. The men completed one of these by the end of October, and the other the following week.[8]

[4] Pollock, General Order Number 2, Cantonment Reno, October 14, 1876, NARS, RG 98.

[5] Captain William S. Stanton, Engineer, Department of the Platte, to Captain Pollock, commanding Fort McKinney, June 3, 1878, gives longitude and latitude of the post flagstaff, NARS, RG 98, LR, Fort McKinney.

[6] Pollock, extensive set of letters and telegrams, Ft. McKinney, Spring, 1878, NARS, RG 98.

[7] Pollock, "Report" to Adjutant General, Department of the Platte, April 15, 1877, NARS, RG 98, LS, Fort McKinney; Pollock, endorsement on letter of his Acting Quartermaster, Lieutenant O'Brien, to Quartermaster, Fort Fetterman, November 7, 1876, NARS, RG 98, LS, Fort McKinney; Adjutant General, Department of the Platte, to Pollock, January 27, 1877, NARS, RG 98, LS, Fort McKinney.

[8] Pollock, "Report," April 15, 1877, cited above; also, check of dimensions on the site by this writer, October, 1962.

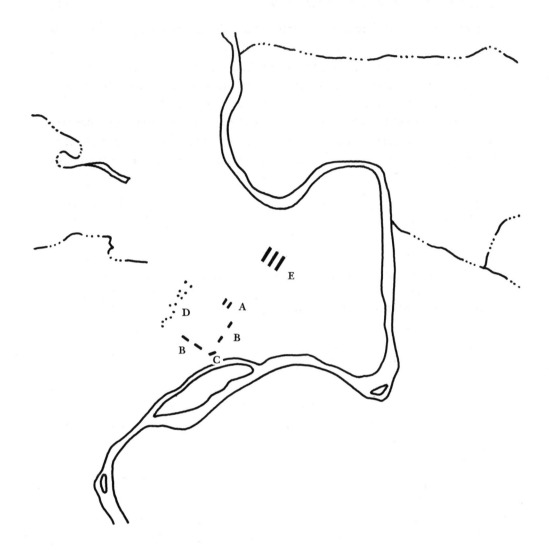

A. Commissary of Subsistence storage cellars
B. Company mess halls
C. Probable hospital site
D. Irregular line of pits, some probably
   sinks and others possibly small dugouts
E. Cavalry stables

Figure 18. The Cantonment Reno (Fort McKinney No. One) site.

Barracks for enlisted men came next. These they made of cotton-wood logs, with pole-and-dirt roofs. These huts are always contrasted with later construction in such a manner that they must have been of simple notched-log construction. They measured fifteen by twenty feet inside. Each of the nineteen huts had four windows.[9]

After completing their barracks, the men built a hospital. Surgeon John E. Summers, then on the staff of the Department of the Platte, visited the post the next year, and left a description of this building:

> The hospital at this station is one log hut, 14 × 16 feet, occupied as a Ward and Dispensary, having a dirt floor and covered with dirt. The height of the roof from the floor inside is 9 feet on one side and 10 feet on the other, giving one foot slope to it; this room has five small windows and one door, and is heated when necessary by one stove. The dispensing of medicines is done in one corner of this room. The kitchen is nearly all (3/4) underground, covered as the hospital, and reached by steps from the opposite corner where the drugs are dispensed. In the rear of the Hospital hut is an old hospital tent, where the office work is done, some Medical Supplies stored, and the Hospital Steward sleeps.[10]

No maps of the cantonment survive in the National Archives, but early surveys, the descriptive record material, and surface evidence make it possible to establish the locations of some structures (see Figure 19). The cellar of modest dimensions at the south corner of the quadrangle is probably the hospital kitchen.

Each company built a mess room and kitchen. These four structures were "half-above-ground," and like the quarters, "well-lighted." Their location is indisputable and is indicated on Figure 19.[11]

Nine huts for officers went up next. Dimensions of these do not survive, but they had two windows each. Four huts for company orderly rooms, fifteen by fifteen feet, followed. Next were offices for the commanding officer, the quartermaster and the Commissary of Subsistence, contained in "two double-huts." Then came a shed and corral, teamster's hut, guardhouse, and blacksmith's shop.[12]

[9] Pollock items cited above, note 7.

[10] Surgeon John E. Summers, "Inspection of the Medical Department at the various posts in the Department of the Platte," September 30, 1877, NARS, RG 98, LR, Department of the Platte.

[11] Pollock, "Report," April 15, 1877, and endorsement, November 7, 1876, NARS, RG 98, LS, Fort McKinney; character of refuse in adjacent middens examined by the author in 1962.

[12] Pollock, "Report," April 15, 1877, and endorsement, November 7, 1876, NARS, RG 98, LS, Fort McKinney.

Commissary Sergeant James Cunningham did not wish to wait for details to complete other structures, so he built his own quarters at about this time.[13]

Last of the early structures was a bakery. All these buildings had dirt floors.

The massive transport needs of the assembling Powder River expedition delayed the arrival of windows, doors, and hardware for some weeks. The last company moved into the log quarters on December 19, 1876. The cantonment at completion of this early construction phase totaled the forty-two structures named above, plus sinks of some sort, not described or enumerated.[14]

The command apparently liked the huts after spending the brisk late autumn days in tents. Pollock at this time described the huts as a "warm and comfortable living place."

This whole early phase of construction at Cantonment Reno required only $931.91 worth of material (doors, windows, hardware, and a small quantity of pine lumber from the Fetterman sawmill). The troops were not given extra-duty pay, and Pollock's quartermaster paid out only $170.00 for civilian employee wages.[15]

The intermittent warfare swirled away from the upper Powder to the northeast that winter, leaving Pollock and his men to spend a quiet winter.[16]

Pollock requested funds in January, 1877, to build a bridge across the Powder. Old-timers had told him that the river crossing at the mouth of the Dry Fork would be impassable during the spring and summer high water, and that without a bridge his supply trains would have to swing off from the trail some distance up the Dry Fork, take the old trail to the crossing near old Fort Reno, and double back up the left bank to Cantonment Reno—an extra six miles of travel. Hearing no more of his request, Pollock then authorized the post trader to build a bridge. This was washed out by the first high water. About March 23, Pollock began construction of a military bridge, using the civilian master mechanic of the post to direct a detail of troops in the work. This sturdy structure, finished on April 6,

[13] Pollock, endorsement of January 9, 1878, relative to expansion of NCO's quarters, Endorsements, Fort McKinney, NARS, RG 98.

[14] Pollock, "Report," April 15, 1877, and endorsement, November 7, 1876, NARS, RG 98, LS, Fort McKinney.

[15] *Ibid.*

[16] Charles Erlanson, *The Battle of the Butte* (Sheridan, Wyoming: privately printed, 1962).

remained in use through the life of the post, and possibly for a while afterward.[17]

Late in May, 1877, the 5th Cavalry regiment took the field in northern and central Wyoming as part of a general policy to interfere with the seasonal hunting and fighting of the hostile Indians. Companies A, B, H, I, and L of the regiment operated in the country around Cantonment Reno and frequently drew supplies from the post.[18] Part of this force set up a tent camp on the Clear Fork, with Captain J. M. Hamilton in command.

Hamilton, on June 16, 1877, designated his camp "Camp McKinney," honoring Lieutenant J. A. McKinney, killed the previous fall in the fight on the Red Fork. Since this was a temporary camp, no one at other posts or higher headquarters took cognizance of the name, but it helped to found the confusion that persists to this day between it and Fort McKinney.[19]

Pollock, on July 23, 1877, formally proposed to rename Cantonment Reno "Cantonment or Camp McKinney." He made this request because his mail was getting mixed up with that of the older Fort Reno, in the Indian Territory.[20] The War Department approved his request, and on August 30, 1877, officially designated the post on the Powder *Fort McKinney*.[21]

The 5th Cavalry withdrew from the field that fall, leaving companies C, E, and M at Fort McKinney.[22] This was long planned. Pollock had contracts out for building materials, had hired some citizen skilled-labor, and put many of his enlisted men on extra duty.[23]

The contractors delivered logs averaging one foot in diameter, cut in twelve-foot lengths, at six cents per running foot. Troop details cut

[17] Pollock, "Report," April 15, 1877, NARS, RG 98, LS, Fort McKinney.

[18] Special Order Number 68, Headquarters, Department of the Platte, May 26, 1877, NARS, RG 98; Headquarters, Department of the Platte, in the field, to Captain J. M. Hamilton, commanding Battalion of the 5th Cavalry, in the field, June 1, 1877, NARS, RG 98; Hamilton to Pollock, June 8, 1877, NARS, RG 98, LR, Fort McKinney; Pollock to Commanding Officer, Fort Fetterman, July 20, 1877, NARS, RG 98, LS, Fort McKinney.

[19] Pollock to Adjutant General, Department of the Platte, July 23, 1877, NARS, RG 98, LS, Fort McKinney.

[20] *Ibid.*

[21] General Order Number 82, Adjutant General's Office, Washington, D.C., August 30, 1877, NARS, RG 98, LR, Fort McKinney.

[22] General Order Number 4, Headquarters, Wind River Command, in camp near Fort Laramie, October 22, 1877, NARS, RG 98, LR, Fort McKinney.

[23] Pollock has a massive volume of correspondence on preparations for construction in the post records of Cantonment Reno from June to October, 1877, NARS, RG 98, LR and LS, Fort McKinney.

roofing poles of minimum three-inch diameter several miles below the old Fort Reno site.[24]

Using these materials, plus hardware, and a limited amount of millwork and cut lumber from the Fort Fetterman sawmill, Pollock's work force built three barracks, three mess rooms, three large cavalry stables, one quartermaster's stable, an additional office, a new guard house, a corn building, and a carpenter's shop.[25] The stables, with their own grain and saddle rooms, were ready for roofing when the cavalry arrived. Shells of other buildings were up, too, and it appears that all the new construction was completed by early December, 1877.[26]

The new buildings were made log-in-panel fashion. Normal space requirements and the size of materials used would indicate that the barracks were twenty-five by ninety feet, approximately. Their location is uncertain, but the large concentration of what appear to be sink locations along the northwest line of the cantonment leads the writer to believe that this was the barracks line.

The three stables for a hundred horses each were located northeast of the quadrangle. They were each about thirty-five feet wide and two hundred and forty feet long. They were made of logs-in-panels and like all the other structures had dirt floors and dirt roofs. Their extensive size and the nature of their occupancy left clear-cut soil evidence of their location.[27]

The first laundresses arrived in the summer of 1877,[28] and some of the noncommissioned officers brought their families to the post that fall. There is little information on the exact nature of their quarters, but they could not have been pretentious, for Pollock took one sergeant from Company C, 5th Cavalry, severely to task for starting

[24] Pollock to Chief Quartermaster, Department of the Platte, June 22, 1877, NARS, RG 98, LS, Fort McKinney; Circular Number 45, Headquarters, Fort McKinney, November 20, 1877, NARS, RG 98; endorsement by Pollock on Post Surgeon's Report, April 26, 1878, endorsements, Fort McKinney, NARS, RG 98; Pollock to Adjutant General, Department of the Platte, May 6, 1878, NARS, RG 98, LS, Fort McKinney.

[25] Penciled draft for an answer by Pollock to a letter of inquiry from the Chief Quartermaster, Department of the Platte, June 21, 1878, NARS, RG 98, LS, Fort McKinney.

[26] Pollock to Adjutant General, Department of the Platte, October 18, 1877, NARS, RG 98, LS, Fort McKinney; Pollock to Adjutant General, Department of the Platte, December 12, 1877, NARS, RG 98, LS, Fort McKinney.

[27] Telegram, Pollock to Adjutant General, Department of the Platte, January 31, 1878, NARS, RG 98, LS, Fort McKinney; draft endorsement cited above, note 25.

[28] Adjutant, Fort Laramie, to Sergeant Scully, Company E, 9th Infantry, June 11, 1877, NARS, RG 98, LS, Fort Laramie.

construction of a twelve-foot by eighteen-foot "jacal" addition to his quarters.[29]

A flagstaff made of two pine trunks cut on the Clear Fork completed the structure of Fort McKinney No. One. This went up about the first of February, 1878.[30]

Dissatisfaction with the squalid earth-roofed huts led Pollock to request a sawmill and to seek a good source of timber. This quest actually led to the examination of alternative building sites, and to the abandonment of the post (see Chapter 10).[31]

Most of Pollock's force had left the Powder River site for the new location on the Clear Fork by July 15, 1878. The post on the Powder (onetime Cantonment Reno, then Fort McKinney) was now designated "Depot McKinney." It had at first a company, then a declining garrison of detailed enlisted men, until supplies of value could be removed. The last of this detail left the depot at the end of 1878. From that time on, only the telegraph station remained active. First it had a sergeant and several privates as a combination detail-in-charge and telegraph repair party. They looked after the buildings, though Pollock had stripped many of them of doors, window sashes, and hardware for use at the new post on the Clear Fork.[32]

Post Trader E. U. Snider had a store building of undetermined nature at the cantonment. He moved with Pollock's force to the new post, and opened a store there. On May 13, 1879, the post commander authorized a Mr. Freron to open a store and eating house (but not a bar) in the old Snider building at the cantonment, and to use one of the cavalry stables.[33]

Major V. K. Hart, in command at the new site, recommended on December 10, 1878, that the government retain a section of land at the old post for use as a camp ground. This was done, and most of the land is still in federal ownership.[34]

[29] Endorsement by Pollock on Sergeant Sayles' letter of January 7, 1878, Endorsements, Fort McKinney, NARS RG 98; Adjutant, Fort McKinney, to Captain Emil Adam, 5th Cavalry, January 7, 1878, NARS, RG 98, LS, Fort McKinney.

[30] Special Order Number 14, Headquarters, Fort McKinney, January 24, 1878, NARS, RG 98.

[31] Pollock's endorsement, April 26, 1878, to Post Surgeon's Report, Endorsements, Fort McKinney, NARS, RG 98.

[32] Pollock's orders and correspondence, Fall, 1878, NARS, RG 98.

[33] Adjutant, Fort McKinney, to Sergeant-in-Charge, Depot McKinney, May 13, 1879, NARS, RG 98, LS, Fort McKinney.

[34] Major Hart, commanding Fort McKinney, to Adjutant General, Department of the Platte, December 10, 1878, NARS, RG 98, LS, Fort McKinney.

The three-man enlisted caretaker detail withdrew late in 1879. From that time on, the army operated only the telegraph there, in the old headquarters building. Usually the telegrapher was a civilian, carried on the payrolls of Fort KcKinney. This station remained open as late as 1883.[35]

The Rock Creek Stage Company received permission in January, 1880, to remove one of the log cavalry stables from the reservation.[36] They built several structures just off the Depot McKinney military reservation to the east, across the Powder and along the Dry Fork. The earliest public land survey shows this stage station.

The records of Fort McKinney No. Two make it clear that all legitimate civilian improvements except the Freron store lay outside the reserved section. Some squatters, characterized as "disreputable persons," occupied some of the military structures and ruins in the summer of 1883.[37] Civilian occupancy centered around the stage station, however. A new iron bridge built by the county, spanned the Powder by 1883. This community, known as "Powder River Crossing,"[38] declined in importance as the railroads approached the Powder River country. By 1886, mail for Fort McKinney left the Northern Pacific at Custer station in Montana.[39] Freight to Buffalo increasingly came from the end of the track on the new Burlington line. The railroad reached Clearmont, just over thirty miles from Buffalo, in late 1892, and the old trail lost most of its usefulness. Soon, even the civilian successors to Pollock's old post on the Powder passed into history.[40]

[35] Record of Events, Post Returns for 1878–1883, Fort McKinney, NARS, RG 98.

[36] Adjutant, Fort McKinney, to Rock Creek Stage Company, November 18, 1879, and January 4, 1880, NARS, RG 98, LS, Fort McKinney.

[37] Adjutant, Fort McKinney, to Sheriff of Johnson County, February 10, 1883, NARS, RG 98, LS, Fort McKinney.

[38] Amanda Hardin Brown, "A Pioneer in Colorado and Wyoming," *The Colorado Magazine*, XXXV, Number 4 (October 1958), 271–283, has much on the Powder River Crossing community and stage station; Ernest M. Richardson, "Iron Horse Wrangler," *Annals of Wyoming*, XXXI, Number 2 (October 1959), 127–139.

[39] Colonel Hatch, 9th Cavalry, commanding Fort McKinney, to Adjutant General's Office, Washington, D.C., October 4, 1886, NARS, RG 98, LS, Fort McKinney.

[40] Colonel J. J. Van Horn, commanding Fort McKinney, to Paymaster General, Washington, D.C., November 29, 1892, NARS, RG 98, LS, Fort McKinney.

Chapter 8. Structural History of Fort McKinney No. Two

The decision to remove Fort McKinney to its new location on the Clear Fork was determined largely by the comparative resources of the two sites, and by the changing nature of army operations at the close of the major Indian campaigns. It will be examined from these standpoints in the following chapters.

Headquarters, Department of the Platte, authorized the move on June 17, 1878.[1] Pollock at this time already had his sawmill at work upstream from the new location on the Clear Fork. He had installed it there with the intention of cutting pine logs and lumber in that area, regardless of the site chosen.[2]

Construction at the new fort falls logically into three periods: an initial, hurried phase to get personnel and offices under cover; a consolidating phase, with some expansion and much repair work; and last, contract work to replace fire losses in the 1890's.

The first phase lasted for about a year and a half, that is, until late 1879. Pollock camped his force above the area under construction at points shown on the Goldman topographic drawing (Figure 19). However, the good construction season was half over by the time they were well settled in these camps.

The early sawmill stood at a point just below the foot of the mountain, convenient to Pollock's source of timber. An old one from the depot at Fort Fetterman, with a boiler too small for its cylinder, the sawmill was incapable of producing enough power to use efficiently

[1] Telegram, Adjutant General, Department of the Platte, to Pollock, Fort McKinney, June 17, 1878, NARS, RG 98, LR, Fort McKinney.
[2] Pollock to Adjutant General, Department of the Platte, January 30, 1878, NARS, RG 98, LR, Fort McKinney.

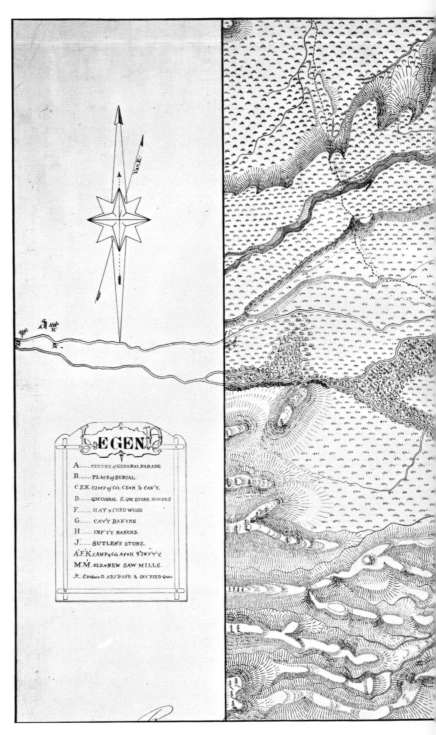

Figure 19. Topographic sketch of Fort McKinney No. Two made by Lieutenant Henry J. Goldman in 1878. (*National Archives and Records Service.*)

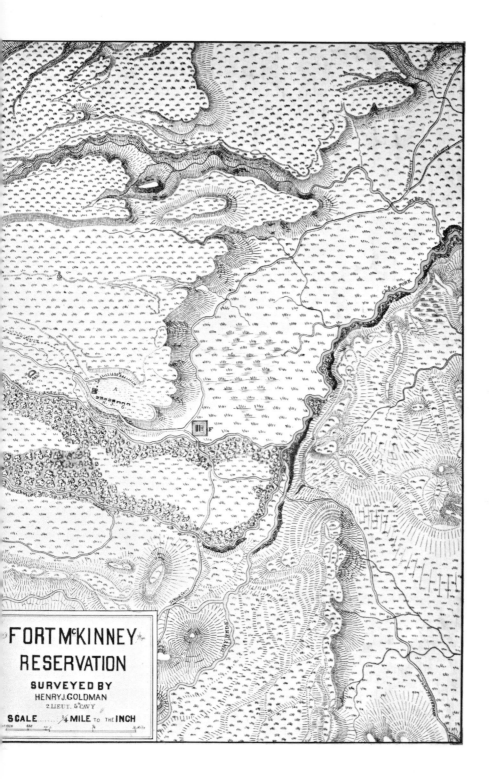

FORT McKINNEY
RESERVATION

SURVEYED BY
HENRY J. GOLDMAN
2 LIEUT. 5 CAVY

SCALE...... ¼ MILE TO THE INCH

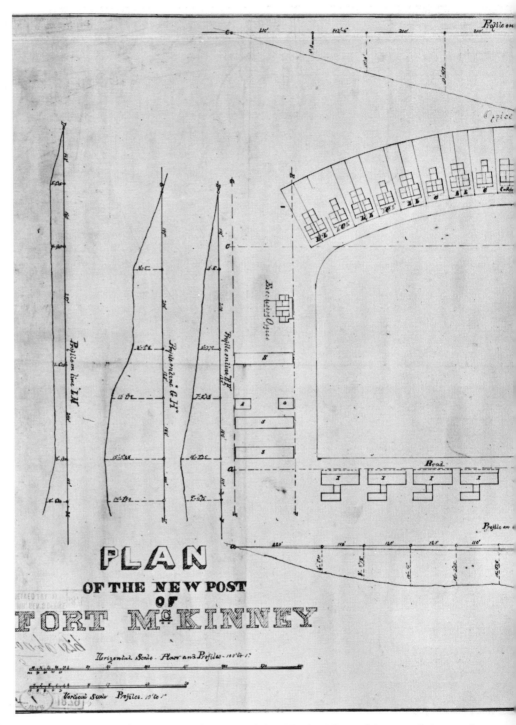

Figure 20. Earliest surviving plan of Fort McKinney, 1879. (*National Archives and Records Service.*)

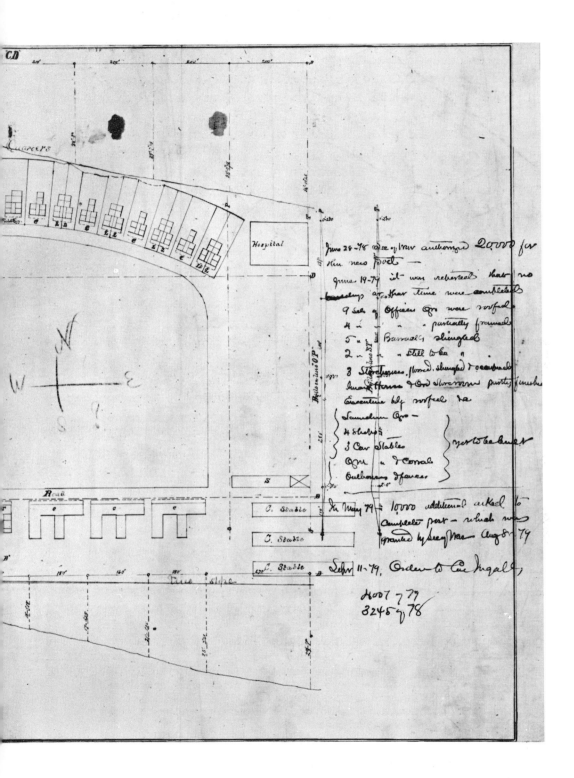

the saws available.[3] For the first six weeks, the men got out some logs, but concentrated on road improvements and bridge building to expedite the movement of logs.[4] Pollock found that a new sawyer got somewhat greater production out of the troublesome old mill.[5] Early in August, he set up a shingle mill. This, too, turned out to be a surplus one from the depot. According to his sawyers, it was one of the earliest types made, capable of only six thousand shingles per day. Pollock requested that the Department Quartermaster buy for the post a late-model machine at a cost of five hundred dollars, capable of producing twenty-five thousand shingles per day.[6]

While the pine on the Clear Fork was infinitely superior to the cottonwood along the Powder, it was not choice timber,[7] and of course there was no time to season it. The ground was steep and rough and Pollock complained of frequent wagon-wheel breakage. He requested an extra supply of front wheels to aid the low wagons in hauling logs on the roughest ground and the steepest slopes. His men kept six grindstones busy, and rapidly wore them out.[8]

Pollock submitted his first proposed ground plan of the post with the estimates made before leaving the old fort. But on location at the Clear Fork, he found that his plan would not fit the chosen ground. The second plan, prepared by Lieutenant Parkhurst, 5th Cavalry, does not survive, but must have had most of the basic features of the plan submitted by Major V. K. Hart the next June (Figure 20). With this second plan, Pollock stated in a general way what he intended to do that fall, and indicated a certain flexibility to accommodate the numbers of men who might arrive:

> I am sorry Lt. Parkhurst did not have the time to make a topographical sketch, showing something of the details of the situation of the post. I do not expect to build this fall more of the Cavalry barracks than the main front building, with the extension which included mess room and kitchen; except recruits should be sent, under which circumstances they could be completed with very little difficulty as the foundation

[3] Furious exchange of telegrams between Pollock and the Quartermaster, Department of the Platte, and the Quartermaster, Fort Fetterman, May and June, 1878, in the Fort McKinney file, NARS, RG 98.

[4] Telegram, Pollock to Chief Quartermaster, Department of the Platte, August 5, 1878, NARS, RG 98, LS, Fort McKinney.

[5] *Ibid.*

[6] *Ibid.*

[7] Notes on the April, 1881, plan of post (see Figure 21).

[8] Telegram, Pollock to Department of the Platte, August 12, 1878, NARS, RG 98, LS, Fort McKinney.

will be laid, the piers built, the sills and joists and possibly flooring laid.[9]

There is no precise month-by-month record of construction progress in this early, hurried period. The beautiful topographic sketch of the reservation by Lieutenant Henry J. Goldman (Figure 19) is our best indication of the extent of construction in early 1879. From the service dates of Goldman and Hart, whose signatures appear thereon, and from other minor data on their activities, this drawing must have been produced between April 15 and June 1, 1879.[10]

Plastering started early in June, 1879.[11] Major Hart, on June 19, submitted the plan of the post mentioned above (Figure 20). This may be similar to the Parkhurst plan, with topographic profiles added and other items updated, perhaps by Goldman. Accompanying this plan was Hart's summary of construction progress to date:

> I have the honor to forward herewith plan of buildings erected and to be erected at post. The storehouse to be built on the east side of post not shown correctly on plan; it is to be on a line with front of stables running back 160 feet.
>
> There are as yet no buildings at the post completed.
>
> Nine sets of officers quarters are roofed, three of them are plastered, the others are ready for the plasterers. Four other sets of officers quarters are partially framed, and paneled to the height of the attic floor.
>
> Five sets of quarters for troops are shingled. Two sets still to be shingled. All to be plastered and permanent floors put in.
>
> Three storehouses are floored, shingled and occupied.
>
> Guardhouse and ordnance store room, shingled and temporary floors in.
>
> Executive building roofed and temporary floor in; occupied in its unfinished condition.
>
> Laundress quarters, four shops, three cavalry stables, quartermaster's stable, and corral yet to be built. One stable is in the process of erection now.
>
> Porches to be built on front of all buildings, length the same as building, width 10 feet.
>
> All outhouses and fences to be built.
>
> All of the buildings are of log, sawed on three sides, rough side to the exterior. East end of post to be left open, in order to more easily increase size of post, by addition of two more companies, should it be deemed necessary.[12]

[9] Pollock to Chief Quartermaster, Department of the Platte, September 16, 1878, NARS, RG 98, LS, Fort McKinney.

[10] Post Returns for the period, Fort McKinney, NARS, RG 98.

[11] Special Order Number 94, Headquarters, Fort McKinney, June 3, 1879, NARS, RG 98.

[12] Hart to Adjutant General, Department of the Platte, June 19, 1879, NARS, RG 98, LS, Fort McKinney.

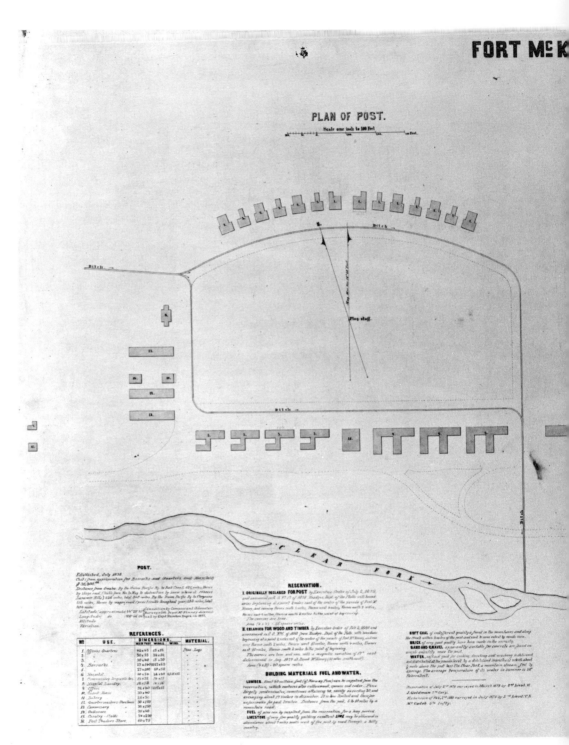

Figure 21. Plan of the post of Fort McKinney, 1881. (*National Archives and Records Service.*)

RESERVATION FOR POST AND FOR WOOD AND TIMBER.

Scale 2 inches to one mile.

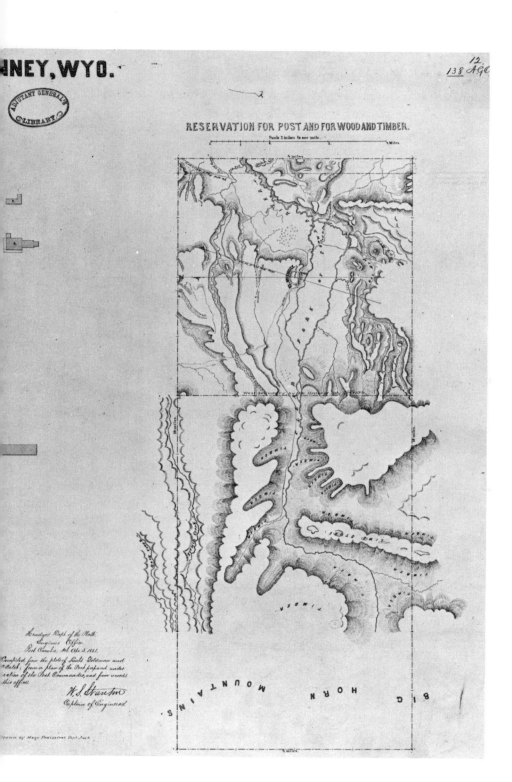

Hart soon requested an allotment of fifteen hundred dollars to build a combination chapel, school, and reading room.[13] This application was refused. While ultimately there were rooms used for these purposes, there was never a chapel, as such, at the fort. The matter did not arise again in official correspondence, perhaps because of the rapid growth of the nearby barracks which were ready for occupancy in finished condition on August 28, 1879.[14]

A special report outlines the state of construction late in October, 1879:

> The post when completed will consist of two sets Field Officers quarters, each containing 9 rooms and a large hall downstairs (also bath rooms) and 3 rooms and hall upstairs, dimensions main building 42 × 45 ft, 9″, L 15 × 25 ft,; 8 sets Captain quarters, each containing 6 rooms and hall downstairs, and 2 rooms and hall upstairs, dimensions main building 40 × 30 ft, L 30 × 15 ft; 16 sets (8 double sets) Lieutenants quarters, each containing 4 rooms and hall downstairs, 2 rooms, hall and small store room upstairs, dimensions each double set, main building 45 × 30 ft, L 32½ × 32½ ft.; Barracks for 3 co's Cavalry and 4 co's Infantry. . . . Executive building 6 rooms, hall downstairs, and 2 rooms upstairs, dimensions main building 40 × 32½ ft, two L's each 15 × 15 ft, 3 storehouses, 2 quartermaster and 1 commissary (cellar under 1/3 of latter) dimensions of each 150 × 30 ft. guardhouse and ordnance storehouse. . . . 3 cavalry stables for 100 horses each, dimensions 270 × 32½ feet. Quartermaster stable and corral estimated capacity for 300 mules and horses; 4 shops (wheelwright, carpenters, blacksmith and saddlers, estimated). Hospital, capacity for 15 or 20 beds. Laundress quarters, (estimated) and rough buildings containing saw, shingle, lath and planing mill. But few buildings at the post are entirely completed—these are yet to be constructed: 2 captains and 4 lieutenants quarters, (2 double sets); 2 cavalry stables, q.m. stable, corral, shop, laundresses quarters and greater part of the hospital—one small wing of proposed building is now being used as a hospital.

The same report further outlined developing problems in the hastily constructed buildings:

> The buildings are constructed of logs, sawed on three sides, rough side to the exterior except the hospital which is frame (boards), outside of the buildings pointed with lime mortar, but owing to the impossibility of "keying," securely it falls out repeatedly, and repointing is constantly

[13] Hart to Quartermaster General of the Army, through Headquarters, Department of the Platte, July 1, 1879, NARS, RG 98, LS, Fort McKinney.

[14] Hart to Adjutant General, Department of the Platte, August 28, 1879, NARS, RG 98, LS, Fort McKinney.

necessary. The officers and mens quarters are plastered inside and the interior finish is most excellent, but owing to leakage between the logs, the plastering gets wet and is thus unsubstantial on the storm side—building material has been procured in the mountains by labor of troops and the construction performed by them and citizen mechanics—none of the buildings are now a year old, but the present condition, owing to unsubstantial foundations, lack of bracing and other causes, is insecure, some of the walls bulge and have to be propped in place.[15]

A special report soon elaborated on building conditions:

> . . . with the exception of the small building used for hospital purposes, there is not a building which has a secure foundation. The sills of the superstructure rest on square pieces of timber placed end-up, these upright supports vary from 6 inches to 5 feet in height and the lower ends rest on small brick piers, resting on the surface of the ground.
>
> . . . .
>
> . . . the frames of the buildings have not in any instance I believe been mortised, the panel logs have not been cleated at the ends to hold them in place, and these defects together with the lack of bracing have rendered some of the mens barracks so insecure that workmen had to vacate buildings during a storm on the night of the 15th ult. Some of the walls of the storehouses and mens quarters are held in place by strong props from the outside.[16]

All these early construction problems must be viewed by the reader with considerable tolerance. The army had under development at the time a large number of posts around the margins of the Indian reservations. Funds were limited, the post themselves were widely dispersed throughout the West, and there were many supply problems for those off the railroad line. Fort McKinney, during this initial construction phase, was two hundred and twenty-four miles from Rock Creek station, the nearest rail point, and nearly two hundred miles from the head of seasonal stream navigation on the Yellowstone.

Soon, administrative paperwork was begun on the second phase, that of finish work, repairs, and supplementary buildings. Available money for such work, from the general appropriation for barracks, quarters, and hospitals, was spread exceedingly thin in the early 1880's. On the northern Plains alone there were ten relatively new army posts in an intensive stage of development, and major construction was also going on at older posts, such as Fort Laramie.

[15] Hart to Adjutant General, Department of the Platte, October 25, 1879, NARS, RG 98, LS, Fort McKinney.

[16] Hart to Adjutant General, Department of the Platte, November 5, 1879, NARS, RG 98, LS, Fort McKinney.

Figure 22. Earliest known photo of Fort McKinney, about 1880–1881. (*National Archives and Records Service.*)

The move for an appropriation, especially for work at Fort McKinney, started in January, 1880, with a request for twenty thousand dollars.[17] Naturally such a request had to be supported by refined plans and drawings. These were not ready until the spring of 1881. By that time the post, as built from the appropriation for barracks, quarters, and hospitals, represented an expenditure of thirty-six thousand dollars, not including the normal pay of the enlisted men who worked on details, but including their extra-duty pay.[18]

Refinements in the planning stages raised the appropriation request steadily to fifty thousand dollars. In 1882, Congress allotted half that much—twenty-five thousand dollars—for use in the 1883 fiscal year.[19]

Two good views of the post between the first and second stages of construction survive (Figures 22 and 23).

The post records do not contain a precise account of the course of construction in 1882–1883. It is apparent from the examination of drawings that most of the appropriation was used to build stables and auxiliary structures of various kinds. Through the same period modifications and improvements of already standing quarters and barracks were made with funds from the usual recurring appropriation for this purpose. Large numbers of civilian laborers supplemented troop labor, with forty-eight persons on the quartermaster's payroll at the peak of construction activity, declining to fifteen by late 1884.[20]

A water system, with a steam pump for pressure, was the last of the second-phase projects to reach completion in 1884. From July, 1878, until the spring of 1880 water was brought from the Clear Fork in wagons. As the weather improved in the spring of 1880, the irrigation ditches built in the fall of 1879 were put into operation, supplying both irrigation and household water seasonally.[21] This water system (see Figure 24) was a much-appreciated major improvement.

[17] Lee, commanding Fort McKinney, to Adjutant General, Department of the Platte, January 7, 1880, NARS, RG 98, LS, Fort McKinney.

[18] Notes on the April 5, 1881, ground plan of the post (see Figure 21).

[19] House Executive Document 1, 48th Cong., 2nd Sess., Pt. 2, p. 225; House Executive Document 160, 48th Cong., 1st Sess., Pt. 2.

[20] Post Returns for 1883–1884, Fort McKinney, NARS, RG 98.

[21] Hart to Adjutant General, Department of the Platte, October 27, 1879, NARS, RG 98, LS, Department of the Platte; Special Order Number 162, Headquarters, Fort McKinney, September 9, 1879, NARS, RG 98.

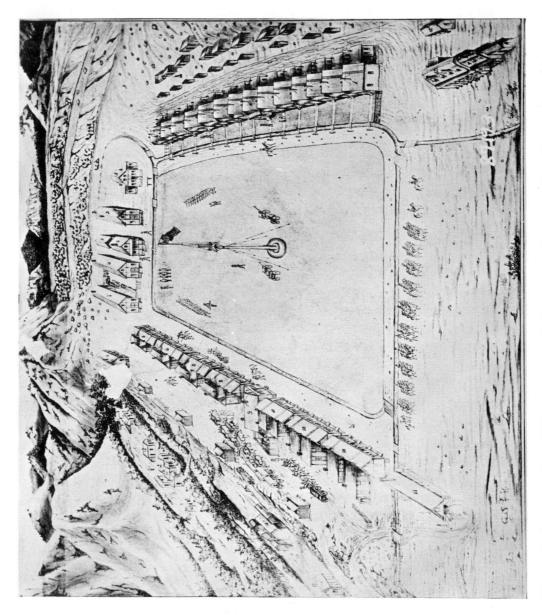

Figure 23. Sketch of Fort McKinney about 1881, by an unknown artist. *(National Archives and Records Service.)*

From this point on, the post was quite comfortable and attractive. The old log buildings still had structural faults and required continual maintenance, but their exterior walls were made weatherproof by the addition of shiplap.[22] Inside, the family quarters conformed generally to the standard plans in use throughout the army. Those for commissioned officers' families were notably spacious and attractive. The barracks were quite good for the period, particularly when compared to some still in use at older posts.[23] A young bride, raised on the High Plains, who visited the post in 1884, was particularly impressed with the clean buildings, the growing trees, and "white clover on the lawn."[24] The stage of the post's development at this time is best shown on Figure 25, and in the Chittenden ground plan (Figure 24). The Chittenden plan can only be dated between 1887 and 1892.[25] Altogether, Fort McKinney No. Two was a reasonably efficient and quite attractive setting for the peaceful and regular garrison activities of the period.

But the layout of the post had one serious weak point—its vulnerability to fire. The buildings stood too close to one another in view of the dryness of the region and the construction material. This was called to the attention of the War Department by General O. O. Howard, Department Commander, in his annual report for 1883.[26] Although the new water supply system went into use in late 1884, it did not alleviate the fire danger. Fire hose requisitioned at the time did not arrive for over a year, and when it did come the connections did not match the hydrants. At no time did the system, even with considerable modification, produce fire-fighting water pressure.[27]

Successive commanders worried often about their post, but with the exception of a small sawmill fire well removed from the post

[22] Annual reports of post commanders, Fort McKinney, NARS, RG 98.

[23] At Fort Laramie, for instance, an adobe barracks was still in use, dating from a quarter-century before. It was in poor repair and crawling with vermin. Post Surgeon's monthly sanitary reports, Fort Laramie, NARS, RG 98.

[24] Amanda Hardin Brown, "A Pioneer in Colorado and Wyoming," *The Colorado Magazine*, XXXV, Number 4 (October 1958), 272–273.

[25] Chittenden's dates of service in the Department of the Platte, from Francis B. Heitman, *Historical Register and Dictionary of the U.S. Army, 1789–1903* (Washington: Government Printing Office, 1903).

[26] Howard, quoted in the *Annual Report of the Secretary of War*, 1883.

[27] Headquarters, Fort McKinney, to Adjutant General, Department of the Platte, December 9, 1885, NARS, RG 98, LS, Fort McKinney; Commanding Officer, Fort McKinney, to Adjutant General, Department of the Platte, September 15, 1885, NARS, RG 98, LS, Fort McKinney; later letters each year same series on the condition of fire-fighting equipment.

Figure 24. Map of the Fort McKinney military reservation, made by Lieutenant Hiram Chittenden about 1887–1892. (*National Archives and Records Service.*)

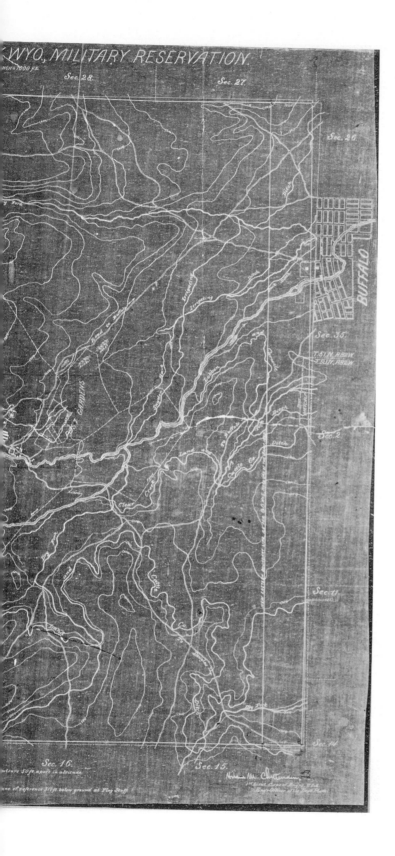

WYO., MILITARY RESERVATION.

135

Figure 25. Fort McKinney about 1885–1890. (*Courtesy of Rev. Stuart Frazier.*)

Figure 26. The two new cavalry barracks built in 1892–1893, shown after abandonment of the post. (*Stimson Collection, Wyoming State Archives and Historical Department.*)

proper, their luck held until May 18, 1892.[28] Colonel Van Horn best describes the great fire at the post:

> The alarm sounded at about 4:20 A.M., and the fire was found to be in the kitchen of the Post Exchange building, where it had made considerable progress when discovered. The entire garrison turned out to extinguish the fire, but the conditions were so unfavorable, the buildings being constructed of seasoned pitch pine logs, located at intervals of only a few feet and as a strong wind was blowing down the row of buildings, that it was found impossible to check its progress. The exchange building was soon a mass of flames which immediately spread to the barracks of Troop H which were to the leeward, and only by great efforts were they prevented from setting fire to the barracks of Company A, 8th. Infantry which were to windward of the exchange building. A charge of 80 pounds of powder was exploded in Troop H quarters and about half the building blown down, but the flames spread before the wind with such rapidity that it was impossible to remove the debris and they passed rapidly over it to the quarters of Troop D, 6th Cavalry. This building burned in a short time, and in attempting to blow it up, Lieutenant Gatewood and Privates Joyce and Schmeig were injured. The fire was communicated to the quarters of Troop B in a short time and this building was soon burning. The cavalry stables were next in the path of the conflagration, but being separated by a considerable interval, the garrison was able, though with the greatest difficulty to save them.
>
> . . . .
>
> At about 1 A.M. on the 20th inst. an attempt was made by an incendiary to fire the quarters occupied by the band, 8th Infantry, but the fire was discovered by a sentinel and extinguished before any damage had been done.[29]

With no cavalry quarters left, Stanton, the Department Engineer, suggested that the cavalry units be transferred to other posts, such as the new Fort Logan in Colorado.[30] The generally unsettled conditions in Johnson County in the aftermath of the Invasion precluded this, however, and contracts were let that fall for new cavalry barracks.[31]

Van Horn found it possible to convert the northernmost of the old stables to a barracks by finishing the interior walls and putting in a

[28] Post Commander, Fort McKinney, to Adjutant General, Department of the Platte, September 1, 1881, NARS, RG 98, LS, Fort McKinney.

[29] Van Horn to Adjutant General, Department of the Platte, May 21, 1892, NARS, RG 98, LS, Fort McKinney.

[30] Exchange of letters between Van Horn and Stanton, Fall, 1892, NARS, RG 98, LS, Fort McKinney.

[31] Endorsement, Post Adjutant, to Van Horn, February 23, 1893, Endorsements, Fort McKinney, NARS, RG 98.

Figure 27. Site of Fort McKinney, 1926. (*Wyoming State Archives and Historical Department.*)

Figure 28. Part of the Fort McKinney hospital, relocated and used as a guest house at the Wyoming Soldiers and Sailors Home. (*Wyoming State Archives and Historical Department.*)

floor and ceiling.[32] This structure housed two troops of cavalry from November 21, 1892, until April 24, 1893, when an accidental fire started, and burned it and the three stables lying immediately south of it.[33]

The new cavalry barracks were completed in June, 1893. These were standard plan, two-story frame buildings, built on contract by a Mr. Jewett. They were light, comfortable, well ventilated, and served well until the abandonment of the post. They drew only the complaint of being hard to heat, even with coal stoves, and nearly impossible to heat with wood stoves.[34]

Additions to the infantry barracks, two new contract-built stables, and a new exchange building were the last construction at the post, the stables being completed in 1894, only a few months before abandonment.[35]

The decade of the nineties was one of great reorganization and consolidation of army facilities and activities. With the Indian problem settled and an interval of peace preceding United States involvement in foreign wars, the army turned toward more efficiently sized training units and appropriate posts to house them. Many of the small frontier posts were abandoned in this era, including Fort McKinney.

Like most of these posts, buildings were disposed of largely as salvage, some evidently before and many after the state acquired the tract in 1903. By the mid-twenties, much of the old post was gone (Figure 27).

[32] Fechet to Van Horn, at post, November 2, 1892, NARS, RG 98, LS, Fort McKinney; endorsement, Van Horn to Stanton, November 7, 1892, NARS, RG 98, LS, Fort McKinney.

[33] Record of Events, Post Return for April, 1893, Fort McKinney, NARS, RG 98; Van Horn to Adjutant General, Department of the Platte, April 24, 1893, NARS, RG 98, LS, Fort McKinney.

[34] Numerous requisitions for stoves and related correspondence, 1893–1894, Fort McKinney, NARS, RG 98.

[35] Annual Report of the Commanding Officer, Fort McKinney, August 15, 1894, NARS, RG 98, LS, Fort McKinney.

Chapter 9. Resources of the Late Posts, 1876–1894

Organization

The late posts had a stable organization. Each post commander was directly responsible to Headquarters, Department of the Platte, in Omaha, Nebraska. Routine correspondence went to the Adjutant General, Department of the Platte, as had the correspondence of Carrington and John E. Smith. Post commanders frequently communicated directly with the Department's Chief Quartermaster and other staff officers on technical matters. There were occasional unit changes. When these occurred, the new units were rapidly fitted into the framework of post activities. Some units had notably long stays at Fort McKinney No. Two (see Appendix A).

Military Personnel

The regular army of the seventies and eighties was noticeably more stable than that of the immediate post-Civil War period. The men came from diverse backgrounds, of course, but there were fewer hangers-on from the volunteer army.

Among the officers left over from the post-Civil War shuffle for positions in the new regiments, the incompetents had mostly been weeded out by the "benzine boards" of the late sixties, had left the army of their own volition, or, as in several notable instances, had become victims of their own incompetence by mid-1876.

Enlisted men were not so often the youngsters full of volunteer tales and unaware of the difference between the volunteer and the regular armies. They signed on for five years, long enough to give pause to the most interested potential recruit. They still got into trouble, as young men in armies will, and they still deserted with high frequency, since desertion had not then acquired the stigma it acquired around the time of World War I.[1] There was a continually smaller percentage of the foreign-born among the garrison of these posts as time went on. Possibly this was due to the changing national origin of the immigrants and to expanding opportunities in the eastern industrial areas.[2] Garrisons were nearly always sufficient for the tasks at hand once the major Indian campaigns ended.

When crash-program building ended at the posts, civilian employment declined sharply, and never reached the peak levels of Fort Philip Kearny. Faster communications and transportation account for part of this, along with a greater tendency to obtain supplies, services, and even construction work on contract. Through the entire period 1876–1894, the employment of teamsters and unskilled laborers declined in relation to the work being done. A fairly stable core of skilled laborers handled such tasks as running the steam power plants, sawing lumber, supervising construction work, and staffing the repair shops. Civilian employee pay throughout the eighteen-year period remained at about the same level while living costs declined sharply, bringing higher real income to the workers.[3]

Other civilians continued to be an important factor at the posts. At Fort McKinney No. Two, most of the nongovernment civilians lived in the adjacent town and did not have the direct impact on round-the-clock post operations as did the people at the early posts. Replacement of the post trader with the post canteen and exchange system in 1889 reduced still further the resident nongovernment civilians at the post.[4]

With peace and increasing stability at the western posts, it became customary for officers, NCO's, and civilian employees to bring their dependents to the forts to live. Most of the officers' families employed servants, who usually resided in spare rooms in the officers' own quarters. The number of such dependents was sufficient to affect many phases of post operations. No attempt is made to identify the many dependents over this eighteen-year period, since the major Indian

[1] Don Rickey, Jr., *Forty Miles a Day on Beans and Hay* (Norman: University of Oklahoma Press, 1963).

[2] Report on this topic periodically submitted by the Post Adjutant to the Adjutant General, Department of the Platte, NARS, RG 98, LS, Fort McKinney.

[3] Post Returns for the period, NARS, RG 98.

[4] Reports of Councils of Administration, managing the post fund, NARS, RG 98, LR, Fort McKinney; Annual Reports of the Commanding Officer, NARS, RG 98, LS, Fort McKinney.

campaigns were largely over, and life for them was much like that for dependents of anyone taking a job in the West. In fact, their housing and other conditions of life at the major posts were usually better than in the typical western town of comparable age.

TRANSPORT

Cantonment Reno opened with transportation facilities not much improved from the time when the old posts were abandoned in 1868. Pollock's mule and bull trains were no different from those of Carrington or of John E. Smith, and the cantonment lived out its day in this condition.[5] Fort McKinney No. Two was largely built under the same transportation handicap as existed in 1868. Both posts did have the great advantage of being much closer to the railroad during their periods of intensive construction—175 and 225 miles respectively, instead of the 750 or more that Carrington had to travel with initial supplies.

The Northern Pacific came up the Yellowstone in 1882–1883, and brought fast mail service within 200 miles from its route. For some time it was the prime mail point for Fort McKinney, with deliveries to the post daily from Custer Station six days a week.[6] The Burlington line crept steadily up across the state from the east, and in late 1892 reached a point only 35 miles from the post (at Clearmont).[7]

COMMUNICATION

The garrison of Fort Fetterman built a telegraph line from the fort to Antelope Springs beginning in November, 1877, and completing the task in January, 1878. Troops from Fort McKinney No. One at the same time connected this line to their own post, with service beginning in mid-January, 1878.[8] The telegraph was extended to Fort McKinney's new site in March, 1879.[9] Stretching 140 miles across the sage-covered hills, tended only at Antelope Springs,

[5] Raymond W. Welty, "Supplying the Frontier Military Posts," *Kansas Historical Quarterly*, VII (May 1938).

[6] Colonel Hatch, commanding Fort McKinney, to Adjutant General's Office, Washington, D.C., October 4, 1886, NARS, RG 98, LS, Fort McKinney.

[7] Van Horn to Paymaster General, Washington, D.C., November 29, 1892, NARS, RG 98, LS, Fort McKinney.

[8] Record of Events, Post Return for January, 1878, NARS, RG 98.

[9] Special Order Number 37, Headquarters, Fort McKinney, February 26, 1879, NARS, RG 98; Special Order Number 48, Headquarters, Fort McKinney, March 24, 1879, NARS, RG 98.

Depot McKinney, and the terminal points, the telegraph was an important but vulnerable link in the posts' connections with higher headquarters. Bad weather, grass fires, and occasional vandalism frequently put it out of order. During the stormy winter of 1886 it did not work at all for several months.

The telegraph line was always maintained by troop labor, in order to keep costs down, and this did not help the reliability of the line. The wire-cutting incidents of the Johnson County Invasion have been much publicized, but the writer is inclined to believe, on the basis of the official records of the post, that the telegraph line from Fort McKinney to Fort Fetterman worked about as well and as often during this famous episode as it usually did under normal circumstances. On May 5, 1893, a new military telegraph line opened from Fort McKinney to Clearmont, 35 miles away, connecting the post with the commercial line that paralleled the Burlington.[10]

FOOD

The army ration itself did not change materially during this period, but the food of the garrisons improved rapidly. Transportation was better. Civil War stockpiles had been used up, issued to Indians, or condemned, making way for a steady supply of newly purchased items at normal and predictable levels.[11] Good storage facilities were the first buildings in use at Fort McKinney's new site, and they continued to be a high priority type of structure. Permanent kitchens, running water, and more regular assignment of cooks within the companies made marked differences. A post bakery made freshly baked bread as needed, and sales from surplus flour and bakery goods went into the post fund for many improvements that could not be obtained with appropriations. Libraries, recreational equipment, "extras" for kitchens, barracks, and other expenditures that were of clear-cut benefit to the entire enlisted garrison came from these funds.[12]

Supplementing the army ration at Fort McKinney No. Two were

[10] Telegraph repair parties total more in number than any other single type of detail sent off the military reservation.

[11] Gordon S. Chappell, *The Search for the Well-Dressed Soldier, 1865–1890* (Tucson, Arizona: The Sun Dance Co., 1964); Sidney B. Brinckerhoff, *Military Headgear in the Southwest, 1846–1890* (Tucson, Arizona: Arizona Pioneers Historical Society, 1965).

[12] Comments in inspection reports; councils of administration; Boards of Survey; comments on buildings, mentioning cooking facilities, NARS, RG 98, LR, Fort McKinney.

the company and hospital gardens. No gardening was done by the army at Fort Reno, Fort Philip Kearny, or at Cantonment Reno-Fort McKinney No. One, for lack of manpower, water, and time.[13]

Major Hart did not try to garden the first season at Fort McKinney, in the spring of 1879. The men were fully employed on construction work, and there was not enough established agriculture in the region to convince Hart it was practical.[14] Captain Jesse M. Lee, in command during Hart's absence in the winter of 1880, with an irrigation system just completed and ready for use in the spring, ordered a large quantity of seed from the D. M. Ferry Company of Detroit, Michigan, emphasizing that he wanted the very best, since this was the first significant attempt at gardening in the region.[15]

The first company and hospital gardens were an outstanding success. Every year until the abandonment of the post the gardens contributed abundantly to the food supply of the post. Cabbages, onions, beets, turnips, carrots, and potatoes were the main crops because they kept well and matured reliably in the unpredictable growing season, subject to late and early frosts.[16]

Better food and better water, supplied by the system mentioned in Chapter 8, meant better health. At the early posts scurvy in winter and diarrhea in summer were regarded as endemic.[17] But by 1885, dietary and water-borne ailments were rare, and the command at Fort McKinney enjoyed health as good as or better than that of the population of the more settled districts.[18]

CLOTHING

There are no complaints in the Cantonment Reno or Fort McKinney records about the quantity or quality of clothing available. Again, Civil War surplus stocks had been used up, issued to Indians, or

---

[13] There is no mention of gardening at the early posts. Carrington took seed along, but did not stay to plant it. Pollock did not garden at the Cantonment Reno site, either.

[14] Hart to Adjutant General, Department of the Platte, January 25, 1879, NARS, RG 98, LS, Fort McKinney.

[15] Captain Jesse M. Lee to D. M. Ferry Co., Detroit, February 28, 1880, NARS, RG 98, LS, Fort McKinney.

[16] Weather records and incidental observations show a range of up to thirty days in individual growing seasons, largely due to the chance occurrence of early or late frosts.

[17] See "Food," Chapter 4. Wishart, "Diary," mentions that intestinal trouble was prevalent that year, as do many to whom it was an incidental problem.

[18] The prevailing complaints shift to respiratory diseases, with a light assortment of common ills. Few men are reported sick on the Post Returns for this period.

condemned by this time. There was more variety, better adaptability, and newer styles to the uniforms of the period, and tailoring facilities were always close at hand. As a result, at Fort McKinney No. Two, in the peaceful years, both enlisted men and officers were able to make a very good appearance on parade or in town. For the sentry or the man on a winter patrol, the buffalo coat, sealskin or muskrat cap and gloves, and good overshoes offered ample protection. These garments were much more weatherproof than those worn by William Murphy on the forage escort trip to Fort Reno, or Grant and Graham on their epic walk to Fort C. F. Smith.[19]

FORAGE

The Indians were clearly on the run by the time forage contracts were made at Cantonment Reno in the summer of 1877. This substantially reduced costs by eliminating the need for a heavy guard force, and cut the risk factor that bidders had to include. It also reduced the wages that contractors had to pay their laborers.

John Hunton furnished the first contract hay of 1877 at $36.90 per ton.[20] Meadows suitable for hay cutting were scattered up and down the Powder in small, uneconomical blocks, and those at the foot of the mountains were far away. High forage costs were an important factor in the relocation of the post. The first contract at the new site a year later was for $13.90 per ton, a sizable difference, amounting conservatively to a yearly saving of eight to ten thousand dollars, and in some years to several times that figure.[21] Better grazing around the new site cut forage needs for several years, but by 1886 the country was heavily overstocked, and even the military reservation had scant grass left. Development of irrigation in this period increased hay supplies, however.[22]

With the advent of agricultural settlements, the army was no longer dependent on corn, which was expensive to freight in. Oats proved to be well adapted to the climate of these valleys, and by the closing years of Fort McKinney, it had dropped in price to $1.75 per

[19] Gordon S. Chappell, *Search for the Well-Dressed Soldier*.

[20] Contract Notification, Headquarters, Department of the Platte, to John Hunton, Bordeaux, Wyoming, July 7, 1877, NARS, RG 98, LR, Fort McKinney.

[21] At the standard ration, for normal garrison of cavalry, assuming a very long grazing season of six months. Active campaigns or bad weather would increase the hay requirements.

[22] Colonel Hatch, "Annual Report of the Post Commander," to Department of the Platte, August 30, 1886, NARS, RG 98, LS, Fort McKinney.

hundred pounds.[23] It was available in quantity, as well. Buffalo entrepreneur Robert Foote delivered *1,200,000 pounds* of oats to the quartermaster at Fort McKinney during the fiscal year 1892.[24]

Luke Murrin of Cheyenne held the last wood contract for Fort McKinney at the old Powder River site, at $5.65 per cord. This was cottonwood, cut on government land, within three miles of the post.[25] At the new Fort McKinney, fuel costs were even lower, for there was a good supply of firewood-quality pine all along the Big Horns. During the early years, some of the abundant mill scrap was certainly utilized as fuel, too. Coal was also used. It was highly variable in quality, and blacksmiths at Fort McKinney used charcoal, bought on contract for as little as $28\frac{1}{2}$ cents per bushel.[26]

The difference in the cost of fuel and forage, and the ample supply of better-quality water (in addition to government use, six irrigation ditches drew water west of the post and crossed the military reservation to civilian land to the east),[27] all added up to huge savings and better living conditions for the sixteen years the new site was occupied. Pollock indeed chose well.

ARMS AND AMMUNITION

Throughout the 1876–1894 period, troops carried the .45–70 caliber Springfield rifle or its carbine counterpart. End products of a breech-loader evolution that began in 1865, these were excellent weapons, as good as any black powder military weapon in the world, and better made and more accurate than most. This design reached a high level of refinement in the 1880's. Springfield Armory pioneered the precise fit of wood to metal that assures good rifle accuracy, and their machine shop operations were among the best in the country. Frankford Arsenal pioneered, too, in cartridge development. These were fitting

[23] J. J. McCullough, Burlington Stage and Express Co., to Post Quartermaster, Fort McKinney, February 15, 1892, NARS, RG 98, LR, Fort McKinney.

[24] Chief Quartermaster, Department of the Platte, to Robert Foote, Buffalo, Wyoming, March 14, 1892, NARS, RG 98, LR, Fort McKinney.

[25] Contract Notification, Chief Quartermaster, Department of the Platte, to Mr. Luke Murrin, Cheyenne, Wyoming, July 25, 1877, NARS, RG 98, LR, Fort McKinney; Pollock to Commanding Officer, Fort Fetterman, January 26, 1877, NARS, RG 98; Pollock to Headquarters, Department of the Platte, February 5, 1877, NARS, RG 98, LS, Fort McKinney.

[26] Pollock to Chief Quartermaster, Department of the Platte, September 5, 1878, NARS, RG 98, LS, Fort McKinney.

[27] Annual Reports of Post Commander on Fort McKinney, NARS, RG 98, LS, Fort McKinney, 1886–1894.

weapons for men who were given the most intensive marksmanship training the world had ever known in the 1880's.[28]

Revolvers were the standard .45 caliber single-action Army Colt, and, less frequently, the fine .45 caliber Smith and Wesson "Schofield." These were the best commercial revolvers in the world at that time, far better, actually, than the concepts of pistol shooting in that period could utilize to efficiency.[29]

Considering the mission of the army at the time, Fort McKinney No. Two had plenty of artillery. The 1879 sketch (Figure 24) shows what may be a twelve-pounder Model 1857 gun-howitzer, the ubiquitous "Napoleon," of the Civil War. We know that they had at least one, possibly several, of the fine little 1.65" Hotchkiss breechloaders.[30] This highly portable weapon could be trailed or packed, and largely replaced the mountain howitzer. Good for direct or indirect fire, it threw a two-pound, high-explosive shell. Direct fire with telescope sight was so accurate on a calm day that there was a fairly good chance of hitting a horse or its rider with deliberate aim at distances up to a mile.[31] It was one of these versatile guns that Major Fechet took along with his column when escorting Wolcott's invaders to the rail line.[32] The post also had two Gatling guns.[33] These were used more for psychological effect, since their effectiveness as tactical fire support for infantry did not evolve until the Spanish War.[34]

[28] Jack Behn, *.45–70 Rifles* (Harrisburg, Pennsylvania: Stackpole, 1956); Elmer Keith, *Big Game Rifles* (Georgetown, S.C.: Samworth, 1936); Kenneth Hammer, *The Springfield Carbine on the Western Frontier* (Crow Agency, Montana: Custer Battlefield Historical and Museum Association, 1959). These books contain a wealth of useful information on the .45–70 caliber Springfield series. The best sources are the *Annual Reports of the Chief of Ordnance*, and the parallel *Ordnance Memoranda* series. The author has had extensive shooting experience with a large number of these rifles and carbines, and is acquainted with a number of other .45–70 shooters. Don't laugh at the "old Trapdoor"; it's a good weapon!

[29] John E. Parsons, *The Peacemaker and Its Rivals* (New York: Morrow, 1950); Parsons, *Smith and Wesson Revolvers* (New York: Morrow, 1957).

[30] See *Reports of the Chief of Ordnance*, 1877–1880. This gun was first used in combat on this continent by Colonel Nelson Miles at the Bear Paw Mountain fight with the Nez Perce in 1877; see orders and reports covering these operations; also, Robert A. Murray, "The U.S. Army in the Aftermath of the Johnson County Invasion, 1892," *Annals of Wyoming*, XXXVIII (April 1966).

[31] Test reports, appended to the *Reports of the Chief of Ordnance*, mentioned above.

[32] See items cited in note 30, above.

[33] Record of Events, Post Return for October, 1894, Fort McKinney, NARS, RG 98.

[34] Harvey Brandt, "Gatling Guns," *Gun Digest* (Chicago: Gun Digest Publishing Co., 1958), pp. 20–29.

The most consistent thing about the resources of the late Powder River posts, then, is the steady improvement in availability and quality of all the materials needed to do the job assigned, which may be attributed to improved training of personnel, to improved selection and transportation of supplies, and to the steadily stabilizing conditions of the frontier.

Chapter 10.   A Resumé of Operations, 1876–1894

Just as the army's mission changed when the Black Hills crisis disrupted the unstable and highly charged policy situation, so it changed again with the defeat and dispersion of the assembled hostile Indian bands in 1876–1877. As the war moved off to the northeast late in the fall of 1876, Cantonment Reno fell more quickly into the new pattern than most of the new Montana posts. By 1878, however, conditions were much more settled over the northern Plains. Troops wintered quietly at the developing posts of Fort Keogh, Fort Custer, Fort Meade, much as at Cantonment Reno. The men now concentrated on improving their living quarters, as time permitted, and keeping communications open and supplies flowing. For several years the cavalry regiments dispersed quickly from winter quarters with the first good grass, moving leisurely but thoroughly over the key parts of the old Sioux and Cheyenne hunting grounds.[1] This kind of patrolling resulted in infrequent action, but steady observation and occasional harassment carried the message to the Indians as nothing else had done. They were forced to break up their old pattern of tribal life and go to the reservations and stay there. This was the clear-cut policy of the day.

Cantonment Reno's function during this time was the monotonous one of a supply and wintering site, not sufficiently varied for extended discussion here. Only once, in the spring of 1878, was Captain Pollock able to break away from the demanding desk work of the cantonment for his own campaign. On the morning of March 29, 1878, he set out with eight officers, 172 enlisted men, Guide Frank Grouard, and twenty Arapaho auxiliaries. The Arapahoes were not enlisted scouts,

[1] Reports of operations of individual units in the field, in the Fort McKinney post records, NARS, RG 98.

but cheerfully went along with Pollock in return for the promise of loot from any Sioux camps they might encounter. The column swung up the Dry Fork, past Pumpkin Buttes, and ran into heavy snow on the trails. Pollock left the wagons of the command with an infantry guard, and struck out with his pack train. They thoroughly scouted the Little Powder and the Little Missouri headwaters, and met up with their wagons again on the Belle Fourche River on April 11, returning to the post on the night of April 14. They saw no Indians, nor any sign that Indians had visited the area since the spring of 1877. Clearly, army operations were working, and the Sioux and Cheyennes were staying out of their old wintering sites.[2]

The 5th Cavalry patrolled the region that summer and fall while the infantry garrison moved the post to its new site.[3] Companies C, E, and K joined Pollock at the new location and stayed during the winter to help build the post.[4]

Fort McKinney was alerted at the time of the Cheyenne outbreak at Fort Robinson in early 1879, and kept its part of the country under observation, but did not field any fighting force.[5]

Part of the post's garrison moved to Rawlins in the fall of 1879, as a reserve at the time of the Ute uprising.[6]

Summer activities shifted from routine patrolling to the new intensive training program begun by the army. This program remained in effect during the 1880's. The troops marched, sometimes over three hundred miles round trip over a period of weeks. They practiced small-unit tactics, marksmanship under field conditions, range estimation, made field fortifications, and engaged in all the other activities that gradually developed the small U.S. army into one of the best trained in the world by 1887. Sighting and aiming drills supplemented the traditional drill at the posts in winter. An intensive season of long-range rifle practice usually preceded the practice marches of midsummer, with chosen marksmen going to the Department rifle camp at Bellevue, Nebraska, for further training and competition. Evening

[2] Pollock to Adjutant General, Department of the Platte, May 7, 1878, NARS, RG 98, LS, Fort McKinney.

[3] Correspondence with Merritt and with Department of the Platte, relative to supplies and troop assignments in the Fort McKinney files, NARS, RG 98.

[4] Post Return for Fort McKinney, NARS, RG 98, 1880–1894.

[5] Special Order Number 46, Fort McKinney, March 12, 1879, NARS, RG 98; Hart to Commanding Officer, Division of the Yellowstone, Fort Custer, Montana Territory, March 18, 1879, NARS, RG 98, LS, Fort McKinney.

[6] Record of Events, Post Return for October, 1879, Fort McKinney, NARS, RG 98.

classes for officers and noncommissioned officers rounded out the training activities.[7]

While the army was thus perfecting its skills, the surrounding country rapidly filled with settlers, and with this change, the army's relationship to the small bands of wandering Indians changed. Crows and Arapahoes still left their reservations to hunt in and along the Big Horns. Old-timers among the whites could be quick on the trigger where an Indian was concerned, and the new settlers were often just scared enough to be dangerous! In this delicate situation the army had to watch the Indians to see that they did not commit depredations, and try to keep them away from the settled areas where trouble could result.[8]

Since the Indians were regarded as a federal problem, sometimes the post commander had to intervene. On one occasion, it was necessary to come to the aid of E. U. Snider, an old-timer and prominent citizen, by assuring Sheriff Frank Canton that it was not necessary for him to arrest Snider for having shot twice (without result) at a Crow Indian who left a gate open after repeated warnings. It is apparent that Snider received some counselling in the matter, too.[9]

On a few occasions, large numbers of soldiers were involved. Troop D, 9th Cavalry, from Fort McKinney spent a month on the Crow reservation around the peak of the agitation stirred up there by Sword Bearer on November 5, 1887.[10] In September, 1888, fifty-five Cheyennes came off their reservation and were escorted back by Troop D, 9th Cavalry.[11]

The Ghost Dance excitement swept over the northern reservation country in the summer and fall of 1890. Guide Frank Grouard, investigating for Major Guy V. Henry, sent in an excellent analysis of the trouble early in October to the Department of the Platte.[12] The Ghost Dance affairs in Dakota brought a quick concentration of force on and around the Sioux reservations there. At the peak of this, only sixty-three soldiers, including the sick and imprisoned, remained at

[7] Reports of training, reports of units in the field, Special Field returns, Fort McKinney, NARS, RG 98.

[8] Abundant correspondence on small incidents and alarms, best summed up in Hart to Department of the Platte, December 14, 1878, NARS, RG 98.

[9] Exchange of correspondence with Department of the Platte, NARS, RG 98.

[10] Record of Events, Post Returns for October–November, 1887, Fort McKinney, NARS, RG 98.

[11] Record of Events, Post Return for September, 1888, Fort McKinney, NARS, RG 98.

[12] Henry to Adjutant General, Department of the Platte, October 30, 1890, NARS, RG 98, LS, Fort McKinney.

Fort McKinney. The Secretary of War authorized the issue of a hundred rifles and five thousand rounds of ammunition to the mayor of Buffalo for "home guard" use.[13]

These, then, were isolated incidents involving considerable numbers of soldiers. There were many incidents and even more alarms caused by the wanderings of the Crow and Arapaho bands over the countryside as late as the early 1890's. Usually, however, it was not necessary to send out troops.

Frank Grouard deserves special mention here. After serving as a guide and interpreter for Crook, he was hired as post guide by Captain Pollock at Cantonment Reno in December, 1877. His pay was $150 per month,[14] and he retained this position and this level of pay until the abandonment of the post.[15] His salary was not a pension for Indian Wars services, as the uninformed will sometimes assert. Grouard's reputation has suffered unfortunately through the clumsy editing and the considerable fictionalization of his "autobiography" by Joe de Barthe, and by the shadow research has cast on the tale he frequently told of his ancestry. Whatever that ancestry was, Frank Grouard shows up in the Fort McKinney records as a good man to have around the post![16]

What did he do there? Primarily, he served as the post commander's eyes, ears, and counselor on all matters relating to Indians. He visited the Crow country frequently and reported what he saw and heard. He kept track of Indian movements in the area. He interpreted for the post commander when Crows visited the post to trade or to beg, as they often did—*190 lodges of them* camped there at the height of the construction season in 1879.[17]

Most of the minor Indian alarms were not answered by a company of cavalry, but by sending Frank Grouard out to talk to them. At the more serious sounding reports, Grouard sometimes took one or two men along, at most. With his considerable knowledge and understanding of the Indian, Grouard usually dispelled the rumor or settled the trouble quietly and efficiently.

[13] A large quantity of correspondence and orders relative to these guns, January, 1891, and January through March, 1892, NARS, RG 98, LR, Fort McKinney.

[14] Post Return for December, 1877, Fort McKinney, NARS, RG 98.

[15] Post Returns and correspondence, Fort McKinney, NARS, RG 98.

[16] Commanding Officer, Fort McKinney, to Frank Canton, August 16, 1885, NARS, RG 98; Henry to Adjutant General, Department of the Platte, October 30, 1890, NARS, RG 98; and other small items.

[17] Hart to Adjutant General, Department of the Platte, July 17, 1879, NARS, RG 98.

From time to time Grouard trailed thieves of government stock. When he did take extra men along, they must have been men of his own choosing, for they were often not the "model soldiers" of the garrison. On the trail of stock thieves in January, 1880, he took Sergeant James Averell and teamster John Cook, and they caught their men far up in Montana.[18]

Grouard served as Colonel Van Horn's principal noninvolved informant and adviser on the events and state of public opinion at the time of the Johnson County Invasion in April, 1892.[19] After the populace on both sides of this complex affair had settled down somewhat, Grouard was one of the three Special Deputy U.S. Marshals who probed the back country of Johnson County to arrest or run off the handful of genuine outlaws in the region.[20]

Grouard was uniformly liked and respected by the post commanders for whom he worked. He was valued not only for his Indian services but for his ability to handle various kinds of civil disturbances, which the army was increasingly called upon to settle in the 1880's and 1890's. The army was a logical choice since many of the states did not yet have efficiently organized and trained National Guard units, and the well-trained regulars of the period had gained a wide reputation for coolness, noninvolvement, and efficiency.[21]

Fort McKinney, because of its remote location, was not called upon often, but in April, 1892, when the cattle-company "invasion" ran aground at the TA Ranch, Acting Governor Amos Barber declared a state of insurrection, and persuaded the President to call the men at Fort McKinney into action. Under orders to stop the conflict, preserve the peace, and cooperate with the governor, Van Horn took a small cavalry force to the TA Ranch and accepted the surrender of the Wolcott party of "regulators" on behalf of the state. They were briefly confined at the fort and then escorted to the railroad by Major Fechet and a cavalry column. Thus ended the Fort McKinney involvement in the so-called Cattle War, although the fires of May 18 and 20

[18] Lee, Fort McKinney, to Commanding Officer, Fort Custer, January 24, 1880, NARS, RG 98; Special Order Number 16, Fort McKinney, January 24, 1880, NARS, RG 98; Commanding Officer, Fort McKinney, to Deputy Sheriff Nicholas, May 3, 1880, NARS, RG 98.

[19] Van Horn to Adjutant General, Department of the Platte, April 11, 12, and 13, 1892, NARS, RG 98.

[20] Statement of U.S. Marshall J. P. Rankin in his report on the Johnson County affair, in Special File 6316–92, "Johnson County Cattle War," Records of the Department of Justice, NARS, RG 60.

[21] Nelson A. Miles, *Personal Recollections and Observations of General Nelson A. Miles* (Chicago: The Werner Co., 1897).

may have been related to that turbulent situation, and the garrison therefore remained on the alert that summer. Officers and men of the garrison were commended for the efficient manner in which they handled their assignments in this situation. A later federal investigation determined that the government probably should not have become involved, but this does not detract from the fine conduct of the garrison in the execution of their orders.[22]

While civil disturbances were on the increase, trouble with the Indians was rapidly ending, and citizens were not long in following the army into the region. As the fort and the nearby town of Buffalo grew up together, a number of scattered and interesting events and relationships occurred. Some of these are worth mention.

Exploring the area in the spring of 1878, Pollock found a family camped near the Fort Philip Kearny site. Hart remarked that these people had tried to raise a crop of potatoes that summer, but that their crop had failed.[23]

Not all the citizens who followed Pollock into the country came to work for the government or to raise potatoes. Assorted whiskey peddlers plagued his command in 1877. They were run off, and sometimes their outfits were broken up and their liquor emptied.[24] Pollock sent word to the battalion of the 5th Cavalry in the field on July 30, 1877, to be on the lookout for "two citizens named respectively C. R. Gahres and Miss Hattie Worley (supposed to be a prostitute)," who were armed with a government rifle and headed in that direction.[25] Pollock also drove off the proprietors of a road "ranche" who located within the reservation on the Dry Fork against his orders, in September, 1877.[26]

Trouble flocked in around the new site. Pollock reported on September 28, 1878:

> . . . a white man has located on Shell Creek at crossing; this man is said is keeping a house of prostitution, the inmates being colored women. I believe he is within the limits of the reservation. . . .[27]

[22] Van Horn, reports and correspondence in the Fort McKinney files; much other material in the Adjutant General's Office; Special File 6316–92, "Johnson County Cattle War," Records of the Department of Justice, NARS, RG 60.

[23] Hart to Adjutant General, Department of the Platte, January 25, 1879, NARS, RG 98.

[24] Special Order Number 98, Cantonment Reno, July 11, 1877, NARS, RG 98; Special Order Number 116, Cantonment Reno, August 6, 1877, NARS, RG 98.

[25] Pollock to Hart, July 30, 1877, NARS, RG 98.

[26] Pollock to "The Proprietors of the Ranche on Dry Fork," September 2, 1877, NARS, RG 98.

[27] Pollock to Adjutant General, Department of the Platte, September 28, 1878, NARS, RG 98.

Confusion attended the construction activity and citizens stole at least one load of lumber from the post in September.[28] A month later citizens were required to obtain permits if they had reason to remain on the military reservation.[29]

The presence of a substantial garrison drew many with the lure of easy pay-day harvests in 1879. The closest of the disreputable "ranches" was O'Dell's. Late that year, Captain Jesse M. Lee, commanding the post, reported a shooting at O'Dell's and stated:

> ... there are several houses of ill fame in full blast just outside of the military reservation on the public highway, but whether that is in violation of the laws of this territory, I do not know.[30]

Citizens were cutting timber illegally on the military reservation the next month, December, 1879.[31] Lee sent an NCO and a private to O'Dell's to retrieve a "Sibley Stove and 5 or 6 joints of pipe" that were supposed to be there, stating that Sergeant James Averell, Corporal Thomas Heeney, and "a woman known as Rosa Lee," knew something about the matter. The quartermaster also reported that there was probably an iron bunk and a heating stove at McCleod's "ranche" six miles southeast of the post, but there was no documented effort to retrieve this.[32]

O'Dell's "ranching" activities came to an end when he was involved in the theft of government property and stock, and headed for Montana. Brought back by Frank Grouard in the spring of 1880, he was released by the federal authorities and left the country.[33]

There was little law and order north of the railroad from the founding of the post until the organization of Johnson County in 1881. Frank Canton, much respected but not universally liked, brought a good deal of stability into civilian affairs during his term as sheriff. Post commanders generally tried to cooperate with Canton and occasionally offered him advice. On one occasion, Frank Grouard

[28] Circular, Fort McKinney, September 27, 1877, NARS, RG 98.

[29] Circular Number 37, Fort McKinney, October 24, 1877, NARS, RG 98.

[30] Lee to Adjutant General, Department of the Platte, November 9, 1879, NARS, RG 98.

[31] General Order Number 96, December 12, 1879, Fort McKinney, NARS, RG 98.

[32] Post Quartermaster to Post Adjutant General, and Post Adjutant General to Officer of the Day, December 14 and 16, 1879, Fort McKinney, NARS, RG 98.

[33] Lee to Commanding Officer, Fort Custer, January 24, 1880, NARS, RG 98; Special Order Number 16, Fort McKinney, January 24, 1880, NARS, RG 98; Commanding Officer to Deputy Sheriff Nicholas, May 3, 1880, NARS, RG 98.

was sent to help him settle a dispute between cattlemen and Arapaho Indians.[34]

Through the early turbulent period, most post commanders had their hands full keeping their own men under control. Only Captain Lee seems to have plagued the civil authorities with complaints about the lawlessness of the region. Subject to rigid discipline and hard work during duty hours and living close to what for a time was a wide-open frontier community, the men let loose when time and money permitted. Although most did not get into trouble, for many others, there are literally volumes of court-martial records of the post which survive as testimony. Most of these specify the more common infractions such as insubordination, drunkenness and fighting, and remaining away from the post overnight without permission.

Occasionally, however, serious trouble arose. Private (once Sergeant) James Averell shot a civilian named Charles Johnson in a brawl in Buffalo in May, 1880.[35] Since there were no territorial or local authorities in the area, Averell was held for federal officers, but released and restored to duty since the offense was not under federal jurisdiction.

Companies of the 9th Cavalry, with all-Negro enlisted men and white officers, arrived in 1885 and formed part of the garrison for the next five years. One company returned to the post toward the end of its occupation. The men were good soldiers in the field and on the parade ground. They had a weakness for frequent and sometimes improbable scrapes, due in part to the fact that the garrison had not only both white and Negro soldiers, but cavalry and infantry units as well.

Some of the court-martial records reveal humorous situations, such as occurred when the 8th Infantry band left a social function at which they had played in town. A wagon had been sent for them at 3:00 A.M., and several enlisted men from the post asked for a ride. Refused by the principal musician, they tried to force their way in. A scuffle ensued, and they were thrown out, following the wagon at a run, hurling rocks and imprecations. They trudged to the post, preceded by word of the altercation, and were arrested on arrival. When brought to trial, the officers of the court acquitted them on technicalities.

[34] Commanding Officer, Fort McKinney, to Frank Canton, August 16, 1885, NARS, RG 98.

[35] Telegram, Lee to Adjutant General, Department of the Platte, May 3, 1880, NARS, RG 98; Lee to Deputy U.S. Marshall Thies, May 5, 1880, NARS, RG 98; Post Adjutant to Deputy U.S. Marshall Thies, May 5, 1880, NARS, RG 98.

Some offenses developed almost standard penalties. Staying in town overnight without permission usually brought a fine of three to five dollars, depending on the frequency of the offense.[36]

Law and order developed steadily in the country. This, along with less time spent on scattered work details, and more time spent in well-supervised training activities, tamed the garrison considerably as time passed. Just as in the civilian community around them, the majority were well intentioned and hard working, and many were much more than just that, in both groups.

Culture arrived early and deserves recognition. Very likely the first school in the county opened in the spring of 1879, conducted by a Mrs. Via, living "in the Canyon." Major Hart ordered parents to send their children to this school, with the quartermaster providing transportation (a sort of "first school bus").[37] The next fall a school taught by an enlisted man opened at the post.[38] In 1882, children of enlisted men could take the spring wagon run by the quartermaster to attend the public school there.[39]

The first mention of the town of Buffalo, as such, in the post records is in a report of November 18, 1879: "The nearest town is a collection of five or six ranches, and is known as 'Buffalo'."[40] From this point on, town and post matured side by side, with many citizens receiving business income or wages from the presence of the post, and with the garrison participating in the varied attractions of the growing town. Army officers participated in the organization of church and lodge groups, and cooperated in social affairs.[41]

Abandonment of the post came suddenly in the fall of 1894, as these moves often did, and caused considerable economic dislocation in the community just at a time when farming and stock raising were undergoing extensive readjustments of their own, and the nation as a whole had not yet recovered from the money panic of the previous year. But

[36] Examination of several hundred records of courts-martial at Fort McKinney, 1878–1894, NARS, RG 98. Sometimes a single field-grade officer maintained steady court-martial for months.

[37] Post Adjutant to Married Enlisted Men of the Command, Fort McKinney, May 20, 1879, NARS, RG 98.

[38] Correspondence with Adjutant General's Office, Washington, D.C., Spring, 1879, NARS, RG 98. Sequence of orders detailing enlisted teachers. Also, Annual Reports of Post Commander, NARS, RG 98.

[39] Circular Number 62, Fort McKinney, September 9, 1882, NARS, RG 98.

[40] Circular, Fort McKinney, December 14, 1878, NARS, RG 98.

[41] Burton S. Hill, "Old Buffalo, Ancient Crow Town," *Annals of Wyoming,* XXXV, Number 2 (October 1963), 1–154; Lillian H. Baker, *The History of St. Lukes Episcopal Church of Buffalo, Wyoming* (Buffalo: privately printed, 1950), pp. 1–8.

Buffalo's settlers and developers were tough, hard working, and resourceful, and their descendants and newcomers have retained much of the same spirit that characterized the best element in the town in its early years. Today the town spreads out steadily over the hills and toward the site of the old post, now, fittingly, a soldiers' home. There are more people, different buildings, a new brand of travelers to serve and shelter, but the mountains and the creek are still there, and an air of history hangs over the place. The modern town is a fitting successor to old Buffalo and to the grand old post on the Clear Fork.

Note on Camp P. A. Bettens, on the Powder near Arvada, Wyoming

This installation does not qualify as a military post, since it was specifically designated as a summer camp of instruction. The camp was the location, from mid-June to mid-November, 1892, of six companies of the 9th Cavalry regiment carried on the rolls of Fort Robinson, Nebraska.

Men from this camp were involved in the Battle of Suggs, which substantially terminated even a nominal involvement of the army in Wyoming's civil affairs that turbulent summer of 1892. Virtually all the action at Camp Bettens is contained in reports on the affair at Suggs in the special Justice Department file on the " Johnson County Cattle War," in the National Archives and in the Adjutant General's Office file on the same events. The latter file is more complete. Copies of all these papers are now on file in microfilm at the Wyoming State Archives and Historical Department, Cheyenne.

Appendices, Bibliography, Index

Appendix A.   Garrison Strengths

FORT RENO (FORT CONNOR)

Aug. 1865	6 Co's, 6th Michigan Cavalry	250*
Sept. 1865	Co's C, D, 5th U.S. Volunteers; Co. A, Omaha Scouts	200
Oct. 1865	"	"
Nov. 1865	"	"
Dec. 1865	"	"
Jan. 1866	"	"
Feb. 1866	"	"
March 1866	"	"
April 1866	"	"
May 1866	"	"
June 1866	" (left early June)	"
July 1866	Co's B, F, 18th Infantry (2nd Bn)	104
Aug. 1866	"	151
Sept. 1866	"	151
Oct. 1866	"	150
Nov. 1866	Co's B, F, G, 18th Infantry	150
Dec. 1866	"	225
Jan. 1867	Co's B, F, I (now 27th Infantry)	225
Feb. 1867	"	225
March 1867	Co's B, F, 27th Infantry	150

Note: There was a gradual decline from about 200 to about 160 from September, 1865, to May, 1866, due to transfers, deaths desertions, etc.

* Figures are approximate for most months, since complete post returns are not available. Approximate figures, based on unit returns and fragmental data, are rounded off.

April	1867	Co's B, F, 27th Infantry	150
May	1867	" "	150
June	1867	" "	150
July	1867	Co's B, C, E, G, 18th Infantry	250
Aug.	1867	" "	250
Sept.	1867	Co's A, B, C, E, G, 18th Infantry	300
Oct.	1867	" "	300
Nov.	1867	Co's B, C, E, G, 18th Infantry	250
Dec.	1867	" "	250
Jan.	1868	" "	250
Feb.	1868	" "	250
March	1868	" "	250
April	1868	" "	250
May	1868	" "	250
June	1868	Co's B, F, 27th Infantry	125
July	1868	" "	125
Aug.	1868	Co's B, F, D, 27th Infantry	200

FORT PHILIP KEARNY

July	1866	18th Infantry, FS&B,* 2nd Bn, A, C, H	252
Aug.	1866	" " " "	343
Sept.	1866	" " A, C, E, H	341
Oct.	1866	" " " "	360
Nov.	1866	" " Co. C, 2nd Cavalry	372

* FS&B signifies "Field, Staff, and Band," F&S signifies "Field and Staff"; other letters are company letters within the regiments. Approximate figures are again rounded off.

Date			Designation				Strength
Dec.	1866	,,	,,	A, C, E, H, K;	,,	Co's C, D, L	389
Jan.	1867	,,	,,	,,	,,	,,	657
Feb.	1867	27th Infantry, F&S,*	A, C, E, H, K;	18th Infantry, Co's B, E, G,	2nd Cavalry,	Co's C, D, L	586
March	1867	,,	,,	,,	,,	Co's D, L	539
April	1867	,,	,,	,,	,,	Co. D	508
May	1867	,,	,,	,,	,,	,,	482
June	1867	,,	A, C, H, B, F, K;	18th Infantry, Co's B, E, G,	2nd Cavalry, Co. D		569
July	1867	,,	A, B, C, F, K	,,	,,		269
Aug.	1867	,,	,,	,,	,,		300
Sept.	1867	,,	,,	,,	,,		300
Oct.	1867	,,	,,	,,	,,		350
Nov.	1867	,,	,,	,,	,,		350
Dec.	1867	,,	,,	,,	,,		350
Jan.	1868	,,	,,	,,	,,		350
Feb.	1868	,,	,,	,,	,,		350
March	1868	,,	,,	,,	,,		350
April	1868	,,	,,	,,	,,		350
May	1868	,,	,,	,,	,,		350
June	1868	Co's A, C, D, I, K	,,	,,	,,		350
July	1868	,,					350

* FS&B signifies "Field, Staff, and Band," F&S signifies "Field and Staff"; other letters are company letters within the regiments. Approximate figures are again rounded off.

CANTONMENT RENO (FORT McKINNEY No. ONE)

Date		Designation			Strength
Oct.	1876	9th Infantry, Co. E; 4th Infantry, Co's B and E; 23rd Infantry, Co. K			160
Nov.	1876	,,	,,	,,	178

Date	Troops	Strength
Dec. 1876	9th Infantry, Co. E; 4th Infantry, Co's B and E; 23rd Infantry, Co. K	185
Jan. 1877	" " Co's B, E, I	171
Feb. 1877	" "	193
March 1877	" "	184
April 1877	" "	170
May 1877	" "	165
June 1877	" "	108
July 1877	" "	129
Aug. 1877	" "	121
Sept. 1877	" "	129
Oct. 1877	" "	128
Nov. 1877	" " 5th Cavalry, Co's C, E, M	298
Dec. 1877	" " "	307
Jan. 1878	" " "	262
Feb. 1878	" " "	203
March 1878	" " "	135
April 1878	" " "	306
May 1878	" " "	358
June 1878	" " "	157
July* 1878	" " " Co's C, E, K	265

FORT McKINNEY No. TWO

Date	Troops	Strength
July 1878	9th Infantry, Co. E; 4th Infantry, Co's B, E, I; 5th Cavalry, Co's C, E, K	265
Aug. 1878	" " "	306

* In mid-July, 1878, Fort McKinney moved to the new site near Buffalo, Wyoming. The July figure represents the garrison strength at the end of the month at the new location.

Date		Strength
Sept. 1878	" Co's B, I	292
Oct. 1878	" Co's B, E, I	304
Nov. 1878	" Co's A, D, F, K, 5th Cavalry, Co's C, E, K	341
Dec. 1878	"	351
Jan. 1879	"	348
Feb. 1879	"	335
March 1879	"	424
April 1879	"	330
May 1879	"	312
June 1879	"	327
July 1879	"	320
Aug. 1879	"	323
Sept. 1879	"	305
Oct. 1879	" 3rd Cavalry, Co's F, K, M	102
Nov. 1879	"	103
Dec. 1879	"	97
Jan. 1880	"	99
Feb. 1880	"	96
March 1880	"	93
April 1880	"	82
May 1880	Co's D, F, K, 3rd Cavalry, Co. A	127
June 1880	Co's A, D, K	108
July 1880	Co's A, D	117
Aug. 1880	"	112
Sept. 1880	Co's A, D, H, I	110
Oct. 1880	"	105

Date	Unit			Number
Nov. 1880	9th Infantry, Co's H, I; 3rd Cavalry, Co. A			110
Dec. 1880	"			125
Jan. 1881	"			120
Feb. 1881	"			122
March 1881	"			119
April 1881	"			115
May 1881	"			110
June 1881	"			105
July 1881	"	Co's A, H, I	Co's A, M	149
Aug. 1881	"	"	"	180
Sept. 1881	"	"	"	175
Oct. 1881	"	"	"	171
Nov. 1881	"	"	"	175
Dec. 1881	"	"	"	175
Jan. 1882	"	"	"	186
Feb. 1882	"	"	"	186
March 1882	"	"	"	175
April 1882	"	"	"	199
May 1882	"	"	"	102
June 1882	"	"	"	146
July 1882	"	"	5th Cavalry, Co's E, I	172
Aug. 1882	"	"	"	142
Sept. 1882	"	Co's A, H, K	"	157
Oct. 1882	"	"	"	170
Nov. 1882	"	"	"	179
Dec. 1882	"	"	"	170

Date				Strength
Jan. 1883	"	"	"	216
Feb. 1883	"	"	"	215
March 1883	"	"	"	215
April 1883	"	"	"	213
May 1883	"	"	Co's C, E, I, L	204
June 1883	"	Co. K	"	189
July 1883	"	"	5th Cavalry, FS&B, C, E, I, L	224
Aug. 1883	"	"	"	223
Sept. 1883	"	"	"	225
Oct. 1883	"	"	"	265
Nov. 1883	"	"	"	257
Dec. 1883	"	"	"	267
Jan. 1884	"	"	"	270
Feb. 1884	"	"	"	267
March 1884	"	"	"	256
April 1884	"	"	"	255
May 1884	"	"	"	264
June 1884	"	"	"	246
July 1884	"	"	"	225
Aug. 1884	"	"	"	231
Sept. 1884	"	"	21st Infantry, Co. A; 5th Cavalry, FS&B, C, E, I, L	294
Oct. 1884	"	"	"	306
Nov. 1884	"	"	"	313
Dec. 1884	"	"	"	314
Jan. 1885	"	"	"	312
Feb. 1885	"	"	"	307

Date	Composition	Aggregate
March 1885	9th Infantry, Co K; 21st Infantry, Co. A; 5th Cavalry, FS&B, C, E, I, L	308
April 1885	,,	305
May 1885	,,	74
June 1885	,,	84
July 1885	,,	78
Aug. 1885	,, 9th Cavalry, FS&B, B, D, E, H, L	382
Sept. 1885	21st Infantry, Co. A; 9th Cavalry, FS&B, B, D, E, H, L	305
Oct. 1885	9th Cavalry, FS&B, B, D, E, H, L	300
Nov. 1885	,,	272
Dec. 1885	,,	285
Jan. 1886	,,	277
Feb. 1886	,,	265
March 1886	,,	273
April 1886	,,	213
May 1886	,,	266
June 1886	,,	265
July 1886	,,	247
Aug. 1886	D, H, L	141
Sept. 1886	,,	155
Oct. 1886	D, H; 7th Infantry, Co's C, K	177
Nov. 1886	,,	172
Dec. 1886	,,	182
Jan. 1887	,,	177
Feb. 1887	,,	170
March 1887	,,	166
April 1887	,,	153

							Strength
May 1887	"	"	"	"	"	"	139
June 1887	"	"	"	"	"	"	147
July 1887	"	"	"	"	"	"	175
Aug. 1887	"	"	"	"	"	"	177
Sept. 1887	"	"	"	"	"	"	195
Oct. 1887	"	"	"	"	"	"	68
Nov. 1887	"	"	"	"	"	"	194
Dec. 1887	"	"	"	"	"	"	197
Jan. 1888	"	"	"	"	"	"	196
Feb. 1888	"	"	"	"	"	"	179
March 1888	"	"	"	"	"	"	177
April 1888	"	"	"	Co's D, K	"	"	174
May 1888	"	"	"	"	"	"	180
June 1888	"	"	"	Co. K; 21st Infantry, Co. K	"	"	178
July 1888	"	"	"	"	"	"	177
Aug. 1888	"	"	"	"	"	"	131
Sept. 1888	"	"	"	"	"	"	179
Oct. 1888	"	"	"	"	"	"	179
Nov. 1888	"	"	"	"	"	"	202
Dec. 1888	"	"	"	"	"	"	204
Jan. 1889	"	"	"	"	"	"	220
Feb. 1889	"	"	"	"	"	"	205
March 1889	"	"	"	"	"	"	204
April 1889	"	"	"	"	"	"	200
May 1889	"	"	"	"	"	"	200
June 1889	"	"	"	"	"	"	200

Date	Unit		Count
July 1889	9th Cavalry, Co's D, H; 21st Infantry, Co. K	8th Infantry, Co. E	153
Aug. 1889	"	"	24
Sept. 1889	"	"	156
Oct. 1889	"	"	155
Nov. 1889	"	"	158
Dec. 1889	"	"	173
Jan. 1890	"	"	169
Feb. 1890	"	"	173
March 1890	"	"	157
April 1890	"	"	168
May 1890	"	"	169
June 1890	"	"	168
July 1890	"	"	151
Aug. 1890	"	"	155
Sept. 1890	"	Co. D	80
Oct. 1890	"	"	114
Nov. 1890	"	"	63
Dec. 1890	"	"	52

(Post Returns for January, 1891, are missing from NARS files.)

Date	Unit	Count
Feb. 1891	8th Infantry, FS&B, A, E, H; 6th Cavalry, Co's C, D, H	310
March 1891	"	309
April 1891	"	323
May 1891	"	296
June 1891	"	299
July 1891	"	285
Aug. 1891	"	254

Date						Co. designation		Strength
Sept. 1891	"	"	"	"	"		"	235
Oct. 1891	"	"	"	"	"		"	255
Nov. 1891	"	"	"	"	"		"	268
Dec. 1891	"	"	"	"	"		"	285
Jan. 1892	"	"	"	"	"		"	277
Feb. 1892	"	"	"	"	"		"	271
March 1892	"	"	"	"	"		"	259
April 1892	"	"	"	"	"		"	186
May 1892	"	"	"	"	"		"	263
June 1892	"	"	"	"	"		"	273
July 1892	"	"	"	"	"		"	229
Aug. 1892	"	"	"	"	"		"	222
Sept. 1892	"	"	"	"	"		"	230
Oct. 1892	"	"	"	"	"		"	229
Nov. 1892	"	"	"	"	"		"	244
Dec. 1892	"	"	"	"	"	Co's C, H	"	232
Jan. 1893	"	"	"	"	"	"	"	234
Feb. 1893	"	"	"	"	"	"	"	280
March 1893	"	"	"	"	"		"	269
April 1893	"	"	"	"	"	Co. C; 9th Cavalry, Co. C		238
May 1893	"	"	"	"	"		"	264
June 1893	"	"	"	"	"		"	274
July 1893	"	"	"	"	"		"	285
Aug. 1893	"	"	"	"	"		"	273
Sept. 1893	"	"	"	"	"		"	274
Oct. 1893	"	"	"	"	"		"	260

	8th Infantry, FS&B, A, E, H; 6th Cavalry, Co. C; 9th Cavalry, Co. C		
Nov. 1893			282
Dec. 1893	"	"	289
Jan. 1894	"	"	290
Feb. 1894	"	"	289
March 1894	"	"	293
April 1894	"	"	280
May 1894	"	"	302
June 1894	"	"	300
July 1894	"	"	159
Aug. 1894	"	"	271
Sept. 1894	"	"	291
Oct. 1894	" 9th Cavalry, Co. C	"	293
Nov. 1894	" A, E, H, K	"	216

Appendix B: Post Commanders

Fort Reno (Fort Connor), 1865–1868

Aug. 1865	James Kidd	Col., 6th Mich. Cav.
Sept. 1865—April 1866	George W. Williford	Capt., 5th U.S., Vol's
May 1866	Edwin Nash	Capt., Omaha Scouts
June 1866	Daniel M. Dana	Capt., 5th U.S., Vol's
July–Nov. 1866	Joseph L. Proctor	Capt., 18th Inf.
Dec. 1866—Jan. 13, 1867	Henry W. Wessels	Lt.Col., 18th Inf.
Jan. 13, 1867—June 1867	Proctor	
July 1867—June 16, 1868	James J. Van Voast	Major, 18th Inf.
June 16–22, 1868	Benjamin F. Smith	Major, 7th Inf.
June 22–30, 1868	James McBride Stembel	2nd Lt., 27th Inf.
Aug. 1868	Jacob Paulus	1st Lt., 27th Inf.
Aug. 1, 1868	George M. Templeton	1st Lt., 27th Inf.

Fort Philip Kearny, 1866–1868

July—Oct. 7, 1866	Tenodor Ten Eyck	Capt., 18th Inf.
Oct. 7—Dec. 1866	Henry B. Carrington	Col., 18th Inf.
Jan.—June 1867	Henry W. Wessels	Lt.Col., 18th Inf.
July 1867—July 1868	John E. Smith	Col., 27th Inf.

Cantonment Reno (Fort McKinney No. One), 1876–1878

Cantonment Reno

Oct. 1876—April 1877	Edwin Pollock	Capt., 9th Inf.
April 12—May 1, 1877	Samuel P. Ferris	Capt., 4th Inf.
May 1877	Pollock	

June 1877   No record for month
June 29—July 9, 1877   Ferris
July 9, 1877   Pollock
Aug. 1877   Pollock
Aug. 1–3, 1877   Ferris

Fort McKinney No. One

Sept. 1877—March 1878 Pollock
March 30—April 13,   Ferris
  1878
April 13–15, 1878   C. J. Von Hermann   Capt., 4th Inf.
April 15—May 1878   Pollock
June 1–3, 5–12, 20–30, Pollock
  1878
June 3, 1878   Wesley Merritt   Col., 5th Cav.
                         Arrived, June, 1878—
                         Intermittent Post
                         Commander

FORT McKINNEY No. Two, 1878–1894

July 1878   Edwin Pollock   Capt., 9th Inf.
Aug. 1878   Albert E. Woodson   Capt., 5th Cav.
Sept.–Oct. 1878   Pollock
Nov.–Dec. 1878   Verling K. Hart   Major, 5th Cav.
Jan. 1879   Emil Adam   Capt., 5th Cav.
Feb.–July 1879   Hart
Aug.–Sept. 1879   Adam
Oct. 1879—March 1880   Jesse M. Lee   Capt., 9th Inf.
April 1880   William B. Pease   1st Lt., 9th Inf.
May–Sept. 1880   George A. Drew   Capt., 3rd Cav.
June 1880   Record missing for
                           month
Oct. 1880   Record missing for
                           month
Nov.–Dec. 1881   Thomas M. Anderson   Lt.Col., 9th Inf.
Jan.–Feb. 1882   Deane Monahan   Capt., 3rd Cav.
March–Aug. 1882   Anderson
Sept.–Oct. 1882   Sanford Kellogg   Capt., 5th Cav.
Nov. 1882—Jan. 1883   Hart
Feb.–March 1883   Kellogg
April–June 1883   William T. Gentry   Major, 9th Inf.
July 1883—April 1885   Charles E. Compton   Lt.Col., 5th Cav.
May–July 1885   Leonard Hay   Capt., 9th Inf.

Aug. 1885—Nov. 1886	Edward Hatch	Col., 9th Inf.
July 1886	Record missing for month	
Dec. 1886—Feb. 1887	James Randlett	Major, 9th Cav.
March 1887	D. W. Benham	Capt., 7th Inf.
April 1887	Hatch	
May 1887	Joseph Garrard	1st Lt., 9th Cav.
June 1887—Feb. 1888	James S. Brisbin	Lt.Col., 9th Cav.
March–April 1888	Benham	
May–June 1888	Brisbin	
July 1888	Eugene H. Dimmick	
Aug. 1888—June 1889	Randlett	
July 1889	John S. Loud	Capt., 9th Cav.
Aug. 1889	Charles J. Stevens	1st Lt., 9th Cav.
Sept. 1889—Aug. 1890	Guy V. Henry	Major, 9th Cav.
Sept. 1890	Loud	
Oct. 1890	Henry	
Nov.–Dec. 1890	Egbert B. Savage	Capt., 8th Inf.
Jan. 1891	Record missing for month	
Feb. 1891—May 1891	Alfred T. Smith	Lt.Col., 8th Inf.
June 1891—Nov. 1894	James J. Van Horn	Col., 8th Inf.
Oct. 17—Nov. 1, 1892	Edmond G. Fechet	Major, 6th Cav.

Bibliography

1. Original Source Materials

Records of the Department of Justice, National Archives, Record Group 60. Special File 6316–92, "Letters Sent and Received relating to the 'Johnson County War,' in 1892 in Wyoming."

Records of The Adjutant General's Office, National Archives, Record Group 94. *General Orders, 1866–1894; Letters Sent, 1866–1894; Letters Received, 1866–1894; Muster and Pay Records,* 5th U.S. Volunteers, 1865–1866; *Special Orders, General Orders, Unit Returns,* 5th U.S. Volunteers, 1865–1866; *Muster and Pay Records,* 18th U.S. Infantry, 1866–1868; *Monthly Rosters of the Distribution of Troops in the Department of the Platte,* 1866–1868. Adjutant General's Document File 29763, PRD 1892.

Records of U.S. Army Commands, National Archives, Record Group 98. U.S. Forces, Kansas and the Territories, 1866, *Special Orders;* Department of the Missouri, 1865–1866, *General Orders;* District of the Plains, 1865, *General Orders;* Department of the Platte (1866–1894), *General Orders, Letters Received;* Mountain District, Department of the Platte, *General Orders;* Fort Reno (Fort Connor, August–November, 1865), November 1865—July 1868, *Post Returns, General Orders, Special Orders, Letters Sent, Circulars;* Fort Philip Kearny, 1866–1868, *Post Returns, General Orders, Special Orders, Letters Sent, Letters Received, Circulars, Communication Register and Endorsements, Wagon Train Books, Quartermaster Records of Persons and Property Hired;* Cantonment Reno-Fort McKinney, 1876–1894, *Post Returns, General Orders, Special Orders, Letters Sent, Letters Received, Circulars, Communication Register, Endorsements;* Fort Laramie, *Letters Sent, Letters Received;* Fort C. F. Smith, *Post Returns, Letters Sent, Letters Received.*

Records of the Judge Advocate General, Special File GCMO–002236, National Archives, Record Group 153.

Bierce, Ambrose G., "Route Maps of a Journey from Fort Laramie-Dakota Territory to Fort Benton-Montana Territory, 1866," surveyor's field book (Ms in the Bienecke Library, William Robertson Coe collection, Yale University).

Wishart, 1st Lieutenant Alexander, "Diary for 1867," unpublished copy of an original in the Glenn D. Sweem personal collection, Sheridan, Wyoming.

2. Government Publications

House Executive Document 1, 48th Congress, 2nd Session, Part 2.
House Executive Document 45, 39th Congress, 2nd Session.
House Executive Document 160, 48th Congress, 1st Session, Part 2.
Ordnance Memoranda (irregularly issued by the Chief of Ordnance, U.S. Army, 1866–*c.* 1900).
Register of Graduates and Former Cadets of The United States Military Academy, West Point: United States Military Academy, 1965.
Report of the Chief of Ordnance, 1866–1894, inclusive.
Reports of the Secretary of War, 1865–1894.
Revised Army Regulations, Adjutant General's Office, Washington, 1861.
Senate Executive Document 13, 40th Congress, 1st Session.
Senate Executive Document 32, 43rd Congress, 2nd Session.
Senate Executive Document 33, 50th Congress, 1st Session.
War of the Rebellion, Volume 48, Part 1, Series I.
U.S. Geological Survey Topographic Map, Fort Reno, Wyoming, 7.5 minute quadrangle, N4345–W10607.5/7.5, 1953.

3. Books

ALTER, J. CECIL. *James Bridger*. Columbus, Ohio: Longs, 1951.
ATHEARN, ROBERT G. *High Country Empire*. Lincoln: University of Nebraska Press, 1964.
———. *William Tecumseh Sherman and the Settlement of the West*. Norman: University of Oklahoma Press, 1956.
BAKER, LILLIAN H. *The History of St. Lukes Episcopal Church of Buffalo, Wyoming*. Buffalo, privately printed, 1950.
BEHN, JACK. *.45–70 Rifles*. Harrisburg: Stackpole, 1956.
BEYER, W. F., AND KEYDEL, O. F. *Deeds of Valor*. Detroit: Perrien-Keydel Company, 1905.
BRADLEY, JAMES F. (editor, Edgar I. Stewart). *March of the Montana Column*. Norman: University of Oklahoma Press, 1961.
BRATT, JOHN. *Trails of Yesterday*. Chicago: University Publishing Company, 1921.
BRINCKERHOFF, SIDNEY B. *Military Headgear in the Southwest, 1846–1890*. Tucson, Arizona: Arizona Pioneers Historical Society, 1965.
BROWN, D. ALEXANDER. *The Galvanized Yankees*. Urbana: University of Illinois Press, 1963.
BRUCE, ROBERT. *The Fighting Norths and Pawnee Scouts*. Lincoln: Nebraska State Historical Society, 1932.
CARRINGTON, FRANCES COURTNEY GRUMMOND. *My Army Life*. New York: Lippincott, 1911.

CARRINGTON, MARGARET I. *Absaraka, Home of the Crows*. Chicago: Lakeside Press, 1950.

CHAPPELL, GORDON S. *The Search for the Well-Dressed Soldier, 1865–1890*. Tucson, Arizona: The Sun Dance Co., 1964.

CROOK, GEORGE A. (editor, Martin F. Schmitt). *Autobiography of General George Crook*. Norman: University of Oklahoma Press, 1960.

DUSTIN, FRED. *The Custer Tragedy*. Saginaw, Michigan: Edwards Publishers, 1965.

EDWARDS, WILLIAM B. *Civil War Guns*. Harrisburg: Stackpole, 1962.

ERLANSON, CHARLES. *The Battle of the Butte*. Sheridan, Wyoming: privately printed, 1962.

FRAZER, ROBERT W. *Forts of the West*. Norman: University of Oklahoma Press, 1965.

FRITZ, HENRY E. *The Movement for Indian Assimilation, 1860–1890*. Philadelphia: University of Pennsylvania Press, 1963.

FULLER, CLAUD E. *The Rifle Musket*. Harrisburg: Stackpole, 1958.

GANOE, WILLIAM A. *History of the U.S. Army*. New York: Appleton, 1932.

GRINNELL, GEORGE BIRD. *Fighting Cheyennes*. Norman: University of Oklahoma Press, 1956.

HAFEN, LEROY R., AND ANN W. HAFEN (editors). *Relations with the Indians of the Plains, 1857–1861*. Glendale, California: The Arthur H. Clark Company, 1959.

———. *The Powder River Campaigns and Sawyer's Expedition*. Glendale, California: The Arthur H. Clark Company, 1961.

HAMILTON, W. T. *My Sixty Years on the Plains*. Norman: University of Oklahoma Press, 1962.

HAMMER, KENNETH. *The Springfield Carbine on the Western Frontier*. Crow Agency, Montana: Custer Battlefield Historical and Museum Association, 1959.

HEBARD, GRACE RAYMOND, AND BRININSTOOL, E. A. *The Bozeman Trail*. 2 vols. Glendale, California: The Arthur H. Clark Company, 1960.

HEITMAN, FRANCIS B. *Historical Register and Dictionary of the U.S. Army, 1789–1903*. Washington: Government Printing Office, 1903.

HYDE, GEORGE. *Pawnee Indians*. Denver: University of Denver Press, 1951.

———. *Red Cloud's Folk*. Norman: University of Oklahoma Press, 1937.

———. *Spotted Tail's Folk*. Norman: University of Oklahoma Press, 1960.

KEITH, ELMER. *Big Game Rifles*. Georgetown, South Carolina: Samworth, 1936.

LASS, WILLIAM E. *Steamboating on the Upper Missouri*. Lincoln: University of Nebraska Press, 1962.

LECKIE, WILLIAM H. *Conquering the Southern Plains*. Norman: University of Oklahoma Press, 1964.

LEFORGE, THOMAS (editor, Thomas Marquis). *A White Crow Indian*. New York: Century Company, 1928.

LUSTYIK, A. F. *Civil War Carbines*. Aledo, Illinois: The Gun Report Incorporated, 1962.

MATTES, MERRILL J. *Indians, Infants and Infantry*. Denver: Rosenstock, 1960.

MILES, NELSON A. *Personal Recollections and Observations of General Nelson A. Miles*. Chicago: The Werner Co., 1897.

MILLIS, WALTER. *Arms and Men*. New York: New American Library, 1958.

OEHLER, C. M. *The Great Sioux Uprising*. New York: Oxford University Press, 1959.

OLSON, JAMES C. *Red Cloud and the Sioux Problem*. Lincoln: University of Nebraska Press, 1965.

OSTRANDER, A. B. *An Army Boy of the Sixties*. Chicago: World Book Company, 1926.

———. *The Bozeman Trail Forts Under General Philip St. George Cooke*. Seattle: privately printed, 1932.

PARSONS, JOHN E. *Smith and Wesson Revolvers*. New York: Morrow, 1957.

———. *The Peacemaker and Its Rivals*. New York: Morrow, 1950.

PRUCHA, FRANCIS PAUL. *Guide to the Military Posts of the United States*. Madison: Wisconsin Historical Society, 1963.

RICKEY, DON, JR. *Forty Miles a Day on Beans and Hay*. Norman: University of Oklahoma Press, 1963.

ROE, FRANK G. *The Indian and the Horse*. Norman: University of Oklahoma Press, 1955.

SECOY, FRANK R. *Changing Military Patterns on the Great Plains*. Locust Valley, N.Y.: American Ethnological Society, 1953.

STEWART, EDGAR I. *Custer's Luck*. Norman: University of Oklahoma Press, 1956.

TOPPING, E. S. *Chronicles of the Yellowstone*. St. Paul: St. Paul Pioneer Press, 1888.

VAN EVERY, DALE. *The Final Challenge*. Volume 4, *The Frontier People of America*. New York: New American Library, 1964.

VAUGHN, J. W. *Reynold's Campaign on Powder River*. Norman: University of Oklahoma Press, 1961.

———. *With Crook at the Rosebud*. Harrisburg: Stackpole, 1956.

VESTAL, STANLEY. *New Sources of Indian History*. Norman: University of Oklahoma Press, 1934.

WEBB, GEORGE W. *Chronological List of Engagements Between the Regular Army of the U.S. and Various Tribes of Hostile Indians which Occurred Between 1790–1890*. St. Joseph, N.J.: Wing Printing Company, 1939.

4. Periodicals

ANDERSON, HARRY H. "A Challenge to Brown's Sioux Indian Wars Thesis," *Montana*, XII (Winter 1962), 40–49.

BRADLEY, JAMES F. "Bradley Manuscript," Book F, *Montana Historical Society Collections*, VIII (1917), 223.

BRANDT, HARVEY. "Gatling Guns," *Gun Digest* (1958).

BROWN, AMANDA HARDIN. "A Pioneer in Colorado and Wyoming," *The Colorado Magazine*, XXXV, Number 4 (October 1958), 271–283.

CARRINGTON, JAMES. "Across the Plains with Bridger as Guide," *Scribners*, LXXXV (January 1929).

GATCHELL, T. J. "Events of the Year 1865 Pertaining to Johnson County," *Annals of Wyoming*, XXVII (October 1955), 141–158.

HILL, BURTON S. "Bozeman and the Bozeman Trail," *Annals of Wyoming*, XXXVI (October 1964), 204–233.

———. "Old Buffalo, Ancient Cow Town," *Annals of Wyoming*, XXXV, Number 2 (October 1963), 1–154.

HULL, LEWIS B. "Soldiering on the Plains," *Kansas Historical Quarterly*, VII (February 1938), 51.

HUTCHINS, JAMES S. "Poison in the Pemmican," *Montana*, VIII (Summer 1958).

McCANN, LLOYD E. "The Grattan Massacre," *Nebraska History*, XXXVII, Number 1 (March 1956), 1–25.

MURPHY, WILLIAM. "The Forgotten Battalion," *Annals of Wyoming*, VII (October 1930), 383–392.

MURRAY, ROBERT A. "The U.S. Army in the Aftermath of the Johnson County Invasion, 1892," *Annals of Wyoming*, XXXVIII (April 1966), 59–75.

RICHARDSON, ERNEST M. "Iron Horse Wrangler," *Annals of Wyoming*, XXXI, Number 2 (October 1959), 127–139.

WELTY, RAYMOND W. "Supplying the Frontier Military Posts," *Kansas Historical Quarterly*, VII (May 1938), p. 156.

5. Newspapers

Montana Post, Virginia City, Montana, July 7, 1866.

The Daily Union Vedette, Salt Lake City, Utah Territory, June 8, 1866; June 24, 1866; June 29, 1866; August 17, 1866.

Winners of the West, St. Louis, May, 1925, p. 3.

Index